hinduism

hinduism

SERINITY YOUNG

Marshall Cavendish
Benchmark
New York

The Early Tradition 9

Developments in Doctrine 17

The Epics 31

Bhakti Movements 47

Marshall Cavendish Benchmark • 99 White Plains Road • Tarrytown, NY 10591-9001 • www.marshallcavendish.us
Copyright © 2007 by Marshall Cavendish Corporation • All rights reserved. No part of this book may
be reproduced or utilized in any form or by any means electronic or mechanical, including photocopy-
ing, recording, or by any information storage and retrieval system, without permission from the copyright holders. • All Internet sites were available and accurate when the book was sent to press. • Library of Congress Cataloging-in-Publication Data • Young, Serinity. • Hinduism / by Serinity Young.
p. cm. — (World religions) • Includes bibliographical references and index. • ISBN-13: 978-0-7614-2116-0
ISBN-10: 0-7614-2116-5 • 1. Hinduism—Juvenile literature. I. Title. II. Series: World religions • BL1203.
Y68 2006 • 294.5—dc22 2005016931 Series design by Sonia Chaghatzbanian • Photo research by Candlepants, Inc.

Photo research by Candlepants Incorporated

Cover photo: Manjunath Kiran/epa/Corbis

The photographs in this book are used by permission and through the courtesy of: *Corbis*: Brooklyn Art Museum, 1, 3,
6-7, 13, 24, 43 (top); 52, 54, 85(lower); Jayanta Shaw/Reuters, 2; Philadelphia Museum of Art, 8; Chris Lisle, 11, 56;
Anders Ryman, 26; Baldev, 34-35; Burstein Collection, 38-39; Arvind Garg, 41; Ravi S. Sahani/Reuters, 43(lower); Bazuki
Muhammad/Reuters, 44-45; Angelo Hornak, 63, 67; Rafiqur Rahman/Reuters, 69; Jeremy Horner, 74; Munish Sharma/
Reuters, 85; Bettmann, 90; Ted Streshinsky, 97. *Art Archive*: British Library, 16, 98-99. *Amirtham/Dinodia Photo Library*:
21. *Art Resource, NY*: Scala, back cover.

Printed in China • 1 3 5 6 4 2

contents

hinduism

Krishna is surrounded by gopis, the wives and daughters of cowherds. In Sanskrit, the god's name means "black" or "dark one."

one

India is an ancient land rich with stories about gods, demons, saints, and kings. The god-king Rama, the playful cowherder Krishna, the divine mother Shakti have all walked the earth and left behind blessings. India is a land where the sacred is never far from sight. And as Indians spread across Southeast Asia to Africa, and in more recent times to the West, faithful Hindus have brought the spirit of their religion with them and have endowed their new homes with it.

What today is called Hinduism is actually a system of religious and philosophical practices followed by various cultural and language groups throughout south Asia—and wherever South Asians have migrated—over a period of several thousand years. In the broadest sense, Hinduism refers to any Indian religious tradition that is rooted in the earliest Indian religious texts, the Vedas—a collection of hymns and prayers that glorify various gods and goddesses. The Vedas also include chants and magic spells that were, and continue to be, recited during sacrifices and other rituals. These writings began to be composed as early as 1400 B.C.E. and did not conclude until around 400 B.C.E.

This time is known as the Vedic period, when male gods dominated and there was a hereditary male priesthood generally referred to as the brahmans. If a father and mother were from brahman families, for example, their children would automatically be members of the priestly class. Those who chose to become priests performed sacrifices to the gods, usually by placing offerings in a sacrificial fire. They also learned the sacred hymns and rituals. These ceremonies were paid for by another hereditary group, the ruler-warriors or *kshatriya*s. These two groups placed themselves above the laborers or *vaishya*s.

Domestic rituals were equally important, and they involved placing small daily sacrifices of grain or ghee (clarified butter) into the household fire. In addition, different regions had their own local cults, with villagers worshipping the goddess of their particular village.

Brahmans

Vedic sacrifices were often elaborate and prolonged rituals that required the participation and expertise of many priests. Priests were named according to their specializations. For example, the *hotri* priest recited hymns. The brahmans supervised the specialist priests. *Brahmans* became the general name for priests.

The vedas

There are four Vedas, the best known of which is the Rig Veda. The other three include hymns taken from the Rig Veda. The Yajur and Sama Vedas are specifically concerned with the technical aspects of sacrifice. The Artharva Veda, which was the last to be composed, is primarily concerned with magic and medicine.

One of the best known hymns from the Rig Veda, is the Purusha hymn, which describes the creation of the world, humanity, the gods, and the social order as a cosmic sacrifice. The sacrificial victim is a huge man called Purusha, meaning "person," from whose body the gods create the world. In the process of preparing the sacrifice, the gods create time by establishing the seasons:

When Gods prepared the sacrifice with Purusha as their offering,
Its oil was spring, the holy gift was autumn; summer was the wood.

A group of men gathers during the Dandajayatra Festival, which is dedicated to the Hindu deity Shiva.

From this sacrifice, the Vedas and all the animals are created. The hymn then asks:

> When they divided Purusha how many portions did they make?
> What do they call his mouth, his arms? What do they call his thighs and feet?
> The Brahman [priest] was his mouth, of both his arms was the Rajanya [warriors] made.
> His thighs became the Vaishya [workers], from his feet the Sudra [menials] was produced.
> The Moon was gendered from his mind, and from his eye the Sun had birth;
> Indra [the warrior god] and Agni [the god of fire] from his mouth were born, and Vayu [the god of wind] from his breath.
> Forth from his navel came mid-air; the sky was fashioned from his head;
> Earth from his feet, and from his ear the regions. Thus they formed the world.

Along with the creation of the world and all its peoples, creatures, and divinities, came the social order. Known as the caste system, it took centuries to develop into a rigid and widespread system.

Vedic religion is primarily concerned with *rita*, the cosmic order that the gods protect and that humans support through sacrifices. *Rita* is represented by the orderly procession of the planets in the sky, the daily rising and setting of the sun, the phases of the moon, the seasons on earth, and the well-ordered society of human beings in which everyone has their place and knows and does what is appropriate for their given caste. So, the farmer should not try to be a warrior, nor the warrior to be a priest.

Despite the great importance of goddesses in later Hinduism, most of the hymns in the Rig Veda are devoted to the male gods who dominate the early pantheon. In the Vedic period, goddesses rarely received ritual offerings, and there are few hymns to them. Goddesses were mainly associated with the earth and water, in contrast to male sky gods such as Indra, the thunderbolt-wielding warrior god. For example, the following hymn from the Artharva Veda praises the goddess of the earth.

> **Upon the earth men give to the gods the sacrifice, the prepared oblation; upon the earth the mortal men live pleasantly by food. May this earth give us breath and life, may she cause me to reach old age!** . . .

The caste system

The caste system further developed the original three-part division of society into priests, warriors, and workers by adding *shudras*, who performed menial and unpleasant tasks for the other three castes. While caste is defined by birth, it is also defined by habit. Members of the higher castes, for example, are vegetarian and do not drink alcohol. Generally, individuals marry within their castes. A family could rise within the caste system slowly, over the generations, by taking on the habits of the higher castes, such as being vegetarian. Individuals could rise by performing their assigned social role (*dharma*) so well, that when they are reborn it would be into a higher caste. It was commonly believed that by conforming to the social order, one was conforming to the cosmic order (*rita*).

Rock, stone, dust is this earth; this earth is supported, held together. To this golden-breasted earth I have rendered obeisance.

The earth, upon whom the forest-sprung trees ever stand firm, the all-nourishing, compact earth, do we invoke.

Rising or sitting, standing or walking, may we not stumble with our right or left foot upon the earth. . . .

May this earth point out to us the wealth that we crave; may Fortune add his help, may Indra come here as our champion. . . .

The earth that holds treasure in secret places, wealth, jewels, and gold shall she give to me; she that bestows wealth liberally, the kindly goddess, wealth shall she bestow upon us!

The earth that holds people of many varied speech, of different customs, according to their habitations, as a reliable milk-cow that does not kick, shall she milk for me a thousand streams of wealth!

Agni, the god of fire, was particularly important to sacrifices since he carried the offerings to the gods. In the following hymn from the Rig Veda, he is praised not only as a priest because of his role in the sacrifice, but as a god who can give blessings and wealth. It was believed that having a priest chant this hymn while pouring ghee into a sacrificial fire would compel Agni to grant wealth and sons. Sons were particularly valued because descent is traced through the male line, and sons perform the funeral rites for their parents.

> **I extol Agni, the household priest, the divine minister of the sacrifice, the chief priest, the bestower of blessings. May that Agni, who is to be extolled by ancient and modern seers, conduct the gods here.**
>
> **Through Agni may one gain day by day wealth and welfare which is glorious and replete with heroic sons.**
>
> **O Agni, the sacrifice and ritual which you encompass on every side, that indeed goes to the gods.**
>
> **May Agni, the chief priest, who possesses the insight of a sage, who is truthful, widely renowned, and divine, come here with the gods.**

The god Vishnu lies on the many-headed serpent in the presence of his wife, Laksmi.

two

The Puranas

Additional descriptions of creation are found in the Puranas, ancient stories about the gods, saints, and kings that were collected from about 300 C.E. to around 1000 C.E. These tales do not differ from the underlying concept of the Purusha hymn. Creation continues to come about through the body of a god. Many Hindu temples around the world display the image of the sleeping god Vishnu lying on the cosmic ocean, floating on the body of a huge coiled serpent. The cosmic ocean contained all the potential of the universe, which began to take shape when it emerged through Vishnu's navel in the form of a lotus, on which sat the god Brahma. The god's body provided all the elements of creation. Similar to the Purusha hymn, the stars emerged from Brahma's head, the gods from his face. His body was the origin of all the things of this world.

Another story also contains the notion that a vast cosmic ocean existed before creation. In this version a golden egg filled with beings floats on the ocean until the god Brahma cracks it open, thus creating the universe.

These stories assume that something existed before the universe: Purusha, Vishnu, or the egg. This means that the potential for creation is eternal, but the universe is not. In Hinduism, creation is actually re-creation. After many eons the universe will pass away, only to be re-created several eons later, again and again.

dharma

Dharma is a complex term with many meanings. It is the law, cosmic and earthly; it is religion and an individual's specific duty; and it is also the specific duties of different castes. Most important of all, *dharma* supports the universe and contributes to a sense of *rita*, or cosmic order.

The Hindu concept of time is one of deterioration and renewal expressed through the four ages. During the first age, right after creation, human beings are virtuous and live long, happy, and easy lives. However, they gradually decline in virtue until the second age when their lives are shorter, sadder, and harder. Conditions worsen during the third age, until finally the fourth age is reached. This is the Kali age, at the end of which the universe will be destroyed, only to be re-created. Then the whole creation process will start anew. Hindus believe we are now living in the Kali age. The decline of these ages is depicted in the decline of *dharma* (duty). *Dharma* stands, well balanced, on four legs in the first age but is wobbling on one leg by the Kali age.

Yet another story of creation, "The Churning of the Ocean," takes place in a sea of milk. According to Hindu belief, the gods and demons are often at war. At the beginning of this story the gods are close to defeat until the great god Vishnu advises them that they need to drink a special nectar to give them the strength to defeat the demons. He tells the gods to throw herbs into the ocean of milk, which they can churn into the nectar. The gods trick the demons, whose strength they need, by falsely promising to share the nectar with them. The gods and demons uproot a mountain, which they use as the staff, with the king of snakes as the rope, to churn the ocean. Vishnu takes the form of a tortoise and descends to the bottom of the ocean to be the support for the rotating mountain. Then:

Out of the middle of the ocean of milk that was being churned by gods and demons, there first arose Surabhi,

source of the oblation, honored by the deities. Both gods and demons were delighted, their minds excited. Even as the heavenly sages were thinking "What is this?" the goddess Varuni appeared. . . . Next appeared the cool-rayed moon which Shiva took as his own, as the snakes took the poison which arose from the ocean of milk. Finally the god Dhanvantari himself came up, clad in white, carrying a water-jar full of the nectar, whereupon all the demons became joyful. . . .

The demons steal the nectar, but Vishnu transforms himself into a beautiful woman who distracts them, enabling her to grab the nectar and give it to the gods, who quickly defeat the demons.

The upanishads

Over time, religions change and grow in response to human understanding as well as to human needs. Public sacrifices could be large events involving many priests, and they drew crowds of people. Often the king and the royal family would be present, and members of the higher castes would also frequently participate. During these gatherings there was time for priests to discuss and argue about the proper way to perform the sacrifices. The events also gave the priests the opportunity to teach their sons, who would inherit the priestly offices, how to perform the ceremonies. The popular belief was that if the sacrifice was performed properly, if each person did the right thing at the right moment—pouring the oblation, chanting the hymn—then the god to whom the sacrifice was dedicated would be compelled to grant the wish of the chief sacrificer. This notion encouraged strict adherence to ritual forms.

Other people, however, came to these gatherings to discuss new religious ideas. Some were people who had taken a more philosophical and mystical view, which led to the compiling of the Upanishads (from the eighth to fifth centuries B.C.E.). One of the main ideas advanced in these texts is that one should turn away from the outer sacrifice of the Vedic rituals to the inner sacrifice of a life of contemplation based on meditation and ascetic practice. The Upanishads undercut the religious authority of the Vedic priests and transferred power to those possessing spiritual insight, some of whom may have been priests, and others who were kings and even women. The word *Upanishad* means "to sit down near a guru." So they are mainly written in the form of dialogues between a guru and a disciple. The Upanishads redefined Hinduism as a personal search for spiritual truth.

The Vedas describe sages and ascetics, mostly men, not all of whom were brahmans, who devoted themselves to serious and highly personal religious practices involving long periods of meditation. The meditators concentrated their minds on one thought alone or just focused on breathing in and out. Ascetics could be very extreme, practically starving themselves to death or practicing "the five fires," which meant standing or sitting completely still, for hours on end, in the middle of four bonfires, the fifth fire being the burning heat of the sun. These men were believed to gain tremendous religious insights and powers from such practices. Individual truth seekers would study with them, questioning them and following their ways. Their ideas and experiences contributed to the Upanishads.

The Upanishads also first introduced the related ideas of reincarnation and karma. Reincarnation means the rebirth of the individual. Karma refers to all of a person's acts and interactions of daily life, which are believed to have consequences in one's present life and which will shape one's future lives as well. These beliefs developed into the notion that everyone is doomed to the perpetual cycle of death and rebirth. Salvation came to mean liberation or release (*moksha*) from this cycle due to knowing reality and not being subject to illusion. In other

A young brahman recites the Vedas in the southern Indian state of Tamil Nadu.

words, through training or "sitting" with a guru, an understanding of reality could be gained.

The basis of all reality, the spirit of the universe, is identified as Brahman, not to be confused with the god Brahma or the priesthood of brahmans. Within each individual there is the Atman, or self, which comes from Brahman and is capable of eternal and blissful union with Brahman. Through contemplation, meditation, or ascetic practices, the Atman can be awakened to this higher destiny. This belief in one principle identified as Brahman marks a radical switch from the belief in the many gods of the Vedas.

In the Chandogya Upanishad, a father teaches his son to understand this idea by telling him to pour some salt into a glass of water. Once the boy does so, the father asks for the salt back, but the boy cannot find it in the glass. The father then asks him how the water tastes.

"Salty," says the boy.

"Well, give me the salt."

The son answers, "I cannot. I can see only water."

Then the father says, "All right, throw it out and come back later." Once the water dissolves, the salt is visible.

The father explains: "In the same way that you did not see the salt and yet it was always there, so too you cannot see the essence that constitutes the self (Atman) of this whole world. That is reality and you are that (*tat twam asi*)."

Through this example of salt and water, the father is teaching his son that Atman and Brahman are one and the same. Although Brahman cannot be perceived, it pervades the whole universe and everyone in it. The part of you that is divine, your Atman, is the divine essence of Brahman.

The public nature of religious discussion at this time is demonstrated in the Bhrihadaranyaka Upanishad. A king sponsors a philosophical tournament, during which one of the philosophers, a woman named

Gargi, questions a famous sage about the nature of reality. Notice that in the sage's response brahmans are respected, but only if they go beyond religious activities such as performing sacrifices, worshipping the gods, or practicing asceticism. The sage asserts that to be truly a brahman one must know Brahman, here called "the Imperishable." Gargi asks:

> "Across what is space woven?"
> He said: "That, O Gargi, brahmans call the Imperishable.
> . . . It consumes nothing nor does anyone consume it.
> "Verily, O Gargi, at the command of that Imperishable the sun and the moon stand apart. Verily, O Gargi, at the command of that Imperishable the earth and the sky stand apart. . . .
> "Verily, O Gargi, if one performs sacrifices and worship and undergoes austerity in this world for many thousands of years, but without knowing that Imperishable, limited indeed is that (work) of his. Verily, O Gargi, he who departs from this world without knowing that Imperishable is pitiable. But, O Gargi, he who departs from this world knowing that Imperishable is a Brahman.
> "Verily, O Gargi, that Imperishable is the unseen Seer, the unheard Hearer, the unthought Thinker, the ununderstood Understander. Other than It there is naught that sees. Other than It there is naught that hears. Other than It there is naught that thinks. Other than It there is naught that understands. Across this Imperishable, O Gargi, is space woven. . . ."

In the Kena Upanishad, the old Vedic gods do not know Brahman, and it is left up to Uma (the goddess of wisdom) to explain it to them. When Brahman appears before the gods, they do not understand what

Buddhism and Jainism

Buddhism began with the life of its founder, Gautama of the Shakya clan. Called the Buddha, a title meaning "the enlightened one," he lived from about 566 to 486 B.C.E. He established a religious community of monks and nuns (monastics) who renounced worldly life. They were celibate, ate only one meal a day, and practiced meditation in order to reach enlightenment. Enlightened beings are released (or liberated) from the endless cycle of birth, death, and rebirth.

Jainism began with its founder, Mahavira (meaning "great hero"), who lived from 549 to 477 B.C.E. He, too, established a religious community of celibate nuns and monks. He taught that divinity dwells within every soul (*jiva*) and that souls could be perfected in order to attain liberation. Jainism's most important practice was that of non-injury (*ahimsa*) of any living beings.

Both Buddhists and Jains also had lay communities, people who took vows not to harm anyone and to live moderately, meditating when they could. They also honored and supported the monastics.

As Hinduism began to define itself, it did so by constantly interacting with these other two traditions. The spiritual authority of the Vedas, for example, was one of the most important elements in distinguishing Hinduism from Buddhism and Jainism, which the latter two religions rejected.

It is. (Brahman is neither female nor male, so the neuter *It* is used.) The gods ask: "What wonderful being is this?" First, they send Agni, the god of fire, to find out what It is, but he cannot, so they send Vayu, the god of wind. He, too, fails. Finally, they send Indra.

He ran to It. It disappeared.

In that very space Indra came upon an exceedingly beautiful
woman, Uma, the daughter of the Snowy Mountain.

To her he said: "What is this wonderful being?"

"It is Brahman," she said. . . .

Thereupon he knew it was Brahman.

Therefore, verily, these gods, namely Agni, Vayu, and Indra,
are above the other gods, as it were; for they touched it
nearest, for these and especially Indra first knew It was
Brahman.

This period of religious debate resulted in the founding of two great Indian religions in the sixth century B.C.E., Buddhism and Jainism. Both challenged the religious authority of the Vedas and of the priesthood associated with them.

The era of the Buddha and Mahavira (see sidebar on page 24) was marked by a political transformation as well. Toward the end of the fourth century B.C.E., the Mauryan empire was established in northern India. Under Emperor Ashoka (who flourished in the third century B.C.E.) almost all of present-day India and Pakistan were briefly brought under one rule. After the decline of this empire, no equally strong central government was established until the fourth century C.E. From about 150 B.C.E. to 200 C.E. India was subject to a series of foreign invasions, which only served to complicate the internal political and religious turmoil that marked those years.

The Laws of Manu

During these centuries of political transformation, the religious tradition of the brahmans was redefining itself. A new class of religious literature was born, which provided detailed instructions

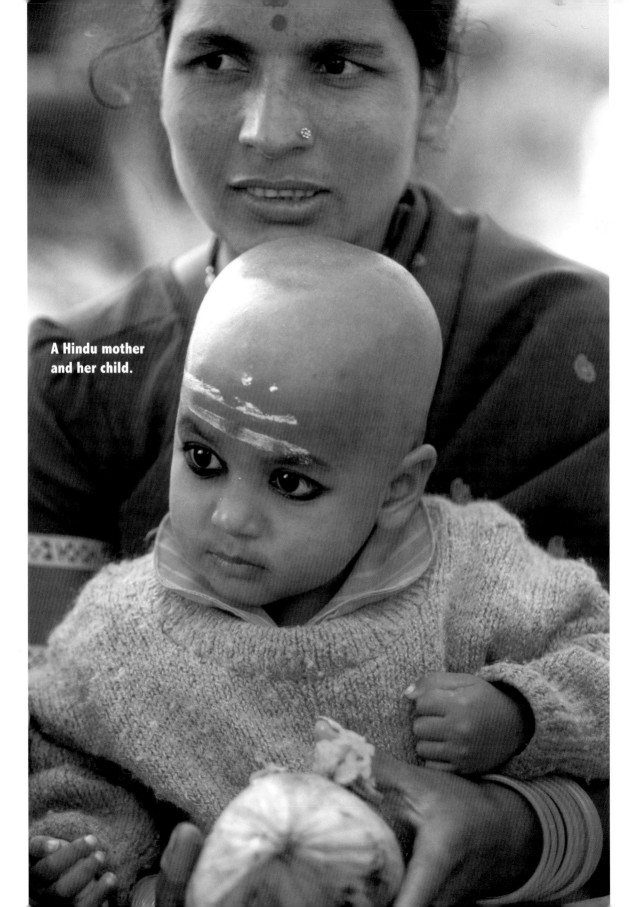

A Hindu mother
and her child.

about how to order one's life. One of the most important texts from this period is the Manu Smriti, or the Laws of Manu. The writing of this work began in the third century B.C.E., and the form in which we know it today was not set until the fourth century C.E. The Laws of Manu reflect a new understanding of salvation (*moksha*), which is to achieve a final escape from the ceaseless cycle of birth and rebirth. This and other new Hindu religious works built on the Vedic notion of an ideal society that would help move people toward salvation.

In Manu's system, each person has his or her own particular duties to society and to their religious goals. The highest caste, the brahmans, are thought to be closest to the gods because they have the time and training to learn the sacred religious chants and to perform the rituals. Because of their involvement in religious practice and their adherence to the doctrine of *ahimsa* (nonviolence), brahmans are also thought to be purer than people of other castes. The duty of brahmans is to perform religious rituals and to study and teach the Vedas.

The *kshatriya*s are considered less pure than the brahmans because their duty to protect others can involve violence. In reality, the two groups depend on each other. The kings and warriors financially support the brahmans and maintain the social order so that the rituals can be performed and the brahmans' sacred knowledge preserved. Along with the *vaishya*s, the *kshatriya*s have the duty of studying the Vedas and Upanishads. The *vaishya*s must farm, breed animals, and trade. The *shudra*s have the primary duty of serving the three higher castes and do not have access to the Vedas. The male members of the three higher castes—the brahmans, *kshatriya*s, and *vaishya*s—are referred to as the "twice-born" because they are considered reborn when they receive initiation as young boys, a ritual denied to *shudra*s.

In addition to the caste system, Manu described the four stages of life (*ashrama*s), when a person is: a student (a period of celibate study); a householder (married with children); a forest dweller (withdrawn from society); and a renouncer (a wandering ascetic).

Each stage of life, from birth onward, has its own traditional religious and social obligations. The religious duties of a student are to study the Vedas, of a householder to perform rituals, of a forest dweller and a renouncer to follow increasingly ascetic paths toward salvation. Salvation is to be attained by fulfilling these obligations in order to reincarnate into the next highest caste. Being born a brahman is believed to make it easier to achieve salvation because the duty to perform religious practices puts brahmans in closer touch with the spiritual life and because brahmans have the highest ritual purity of all the castes. In reality, though, most people never go beyond the householder stage, which is often described as the most important stage. Hinduism actually celebrates this stage of life.

The Laws of Manu are a male-oriented system in which women are mainly limited to the stage of the householder. Their education takes place at home, under the supervision of the women of the family, and is directed toward the household tasks they will perform as wives and mothers. Eventually, Hindu women were encouraged to think of their husbands as their gods; the women were, quite literally, to devote themselves to their husbands. Women were, however, viewed as goddesses in certain rituals and as the goddess Laksmi, the bringer of prosperity, into the home. This points to the fluid boundaries between human and divine in Hinduism where the gods are very human and some humans, especially ascetic sages, achieve godlike status.

The four stages of life were interwoven with caste, so the whole system was limited to members of the first three castes, within which each caste had its own *dharma* during the different stages. The *dharma* of the *shurda*s was to serve the other castes.

It was also believed that a fully integrated life involved the pursuits of four goals (*artha*s): *artha*, material pursuits; *kama*, pleasure or love; *dharma*, duty; and *moksha*, salvation. The first three are focused on the householder stage. The fourth stage, salvation—although it should be a concern throughout life—is primarily the goal of those in the fourth stage of life, the renouncers.

Most great religious traditions formulate law books, which are idealized representations of how things should be. The Laws of Manu was, and is, consulted by orthodox Hindus when they are in doubt about correct procedure. This text organizes the system of Hindu religious law in all aspects of daily life. It expresses the Hindu belief that each person, animal, and plant is sacred and has a unique *dharma* that must be fulfilled so that cosmic order can triumph and the gods' creation can be maintained.

Marriage ceremony

Since most Hindus live out their lives in the householder stage, marriage is an important ceremony. According to the Vedas, a man is complete, or is capable of performing a sacrifice, only after obtaining a wife and having a son. Hindu weddings are joyous events that take place for several days, during which the bride's family spares no expense. The ceremonies surrounding the marriage vary from region to region and among castes; what follows is a general description. It is still common for parents to choose the partners of their children and to negotiate the terms of the marriage, particularly the bride's dowry. Often the horoscopes of the bride and the groom are consulted to see whether the couple will be compatible.

There are preliminary ceremonies at both the bride's house and the groom's. The women of both families repeatedly anoint (rub oil onto) the bride and groom as if they were deities. Indeed, they are treated as such during the wedding and are dressed in the royal clothes and ornaments associated with the gods. Since the marriage ceremony takes place at the bride's house, the groom travels there—preferably on horseback and accompanied by a musical band and his male relatives. The journey is timed so that the groom arrives in the evening. Just outside the village, the bride's relatives formally greet the groom's party and guide them to where they will stay during the wedding. Once the groom appears, the bride's relatives wash the feet of the groom and his party (a traditional act of hospitality) and offer them refreshments. The groom then enters the bride's house to offer his respects to her family. During this visit, there is a great deal of joking and teasing, especially by the bride's younger sisters, and a good deal of off-color humor takes place.

The next day, or the day after, the groom returns to the bride's house for the final ceremony, which is held in a small marriage pavilion erected for the occasion. The faces of both the bride and the groom are veiled, and relatives tie the ends of their clothes together. The groom then leads the bride around the outside of the pavilion several times. Usually they complete seven circles. Among the higher castes it is considered ideal to have a brahman priest present. After these circumambulations, the bride and groom sit together, with the bride on the groom's left side. The parents of the bride wash the feet of the couple and apply *tilak*s, lucky red marks made of rice and turmeric, to their foreheads. Often the family gods are worshipped, and then there is the most elaborate feast the bride's family can afford.

The next day the newly married couple leaves for the groom's house, where they will usually live, and where a new round of ceremonies takes place to welcome the bride and pray for the couple's fertility.

three

THE EPICS

Another form of literature are the epics, especially the Mahabharata (composed between the fifth century B.C.E. and the fourth century C.E.) and the Ramayana (composed around the second century B.C.E.). These texts contain some of the best known Hindu stories, legends, and myths. Besides being artistic and entertaining, these tales provide guidelines for appropriate social and religious behavior. The stories use villains to illustrate the consequences of improper or un-dharmic behavior as well as heroes and heroines to depict all that is noble and dharmic as both experience highly dramatic events such as exile and war. The epics show people at the four stages of life as they pursue the four goals of life. The Mahabharata and the Ramayana were and continue to be publicly recited, sung, and performed all over south Asia, and wherever Hindus have immigrated. All Hindus know these stories. Consequently, they are two of the main means of communicating the values of Hinduism. More than anything else, they have given India a common cultural base and unity.

The epics are stories about exile, in which the heroes are forced to leave their homes and wander throughout India. In this way, the Mahabharata and the Ramayana are great geographical sagas in which the heroes battle demons—who were perhaps the tribal gods of people not influenced by the religion of the brahmans—and they make many places holy by their presence. The epics were important parts of the process of Hinduizing India because they turned the Indian landscape into a vast network of sacred sites, holy cities, and rivers that were visited by heroic and divine beings. Faithful Hindus often undertake pilgrimages to such places. Indeed, a long section in book three of the Mahabharata, the Book of the Forest, has the heroes visiting pilgrimage sites and discussing the virtues that could be obtained from them.

Both works focus on Vishnu, through his incarnations (embodiments of gods in human form), Rama and Krishna. The god Shiva is also present in these texts and is shown as complementary to Vishnu. Vishnu is the preserver of the universe, and Shiva is the destroyer. Brahma, the creator, is also present, as is the Goddess in her many forms. The Mahabharata and the Ramayana respect all earlier forms of religious practice: sacrifice, asceticism, and the search for spiritual knowledge. These are accepted but are defined as incomplete without *bhakti* (devotion). Without devotion to god, no religious act is meaningful.

The gods incarnate on earth in times of crisis, when *dharma* is in danger. This is especially the role of Vishnu as the preserver of the universe. By incarnating, he re-establishes order, maintaining the caste system and the stages of life as the supports of universal order.

The Mahabharata

The Mahabharata is a huge text divided into eighteen books. It is held together by the story of the five Pandava brothers—who are the heroes of the epic—and their joint wife, Draupadi. The Pandavas practiced an unusual form of marriage called polyandry (*poly* means "many," and *andr* means "man") in which one woman has several husbands. This form of marriage exists in the Himalayas and in Tibet. Normally, Hindu marriages are monogamous, involving one wife and one husband. The central event of the Mahabharata is a great civil war between cousins for the right to rule. Through this conflict, the work emphasizes the importance of sons, the nature of the gods, the power of asceticism, and the proper role of kingship. Things begin to go wrong for the Pandavas when the oldest brother, Yudisthira, is challenged to a game of dice by his cousin Duryodhana. Yudisthira looses all restraint and gambles away everything he has, including himself, his four brothers, and their wife, Draupadi. Duryodhana, the victor, demands that Draupadi be brought into the hall of the kings. When confronted, Draupadi shows her knowledge of the law (*dharma*) by asking whether her husband had first lost his own freedom before gambling away hers. She argues that having first lost himself, he had lost the right to use her as a stake, because a slave cannot own anyone else. She loses the argument, but Duryodhana's father, a great king, offers her a boon—a gift that cannot be refused. She asks for the release of Yudisthira. The king offers her another boon. She asks for the release of the four other brothers. She refuses a third boon, saying it is not proper for a *kshatriya* to receive more than two boons. The king praises her as the most dharmic of women and frees her.

Through Draupadi, the Pandava brothers are saved from slavery, but they are exiled for twelve years. Once in the forest, they have many opportunities to prove their heroic natures, both as warriors against demons and as men who follow *dharma*. At the end of their exile, the Pandavas are forced into a great and destructive civil war by their cousin Duryodhana, who wants to be king.

The proper behavior of kings is an important element in the epics. As early as the sixth century B.C.E. a dharmic king began to be defined as a king whose main duty was to rule according to *dharma* so that the social order could be maintained and *dharma* could flourish. In other words, the king's role was to keep society functioning as it was divinely ordained by the original sacrifice of Purusha, which means maintaining the caste system. In large part, this idea of kingship was shaped by Emperor Ashoka, who conquered almost all of present-day India. He was instrumental in the spread of Buddhism, which he used to unify his far-flung and diverse empire. Importantly, Ashoka referred to Buddhism as *dharma*, a term that was acceptable and meaningful to people belonging to all of India's religions: Hinduism, Buddhism, Jainism, and others. He established peace in his diverse kingdom, brought the government administration in line with Buddhist principles, and had Buddhism preached to the people. Most signicantantly, he ordered the various religious groups to respect one another. He erected many pillars throughout his kingdom that had his edicts carved into them. The idea of the dharmic king endured into modern times, and the wheel that Emperor Ashoka used to symbolize *dharma* on one of his pillars is depicted on the flag of modern democratic India.

In the following excerpt from the Mahabharata, Yudisthira—the oldest of the Pandavas and the rightful king—questions Bhishma, a highly respected elder statesman,

Kathakali dancers from Kerala in south India enact a scene from the Mahabharata.

about the proper duty of the king. In this dialogue, *anarchy* means "the absence of *dharma* and the caste system."

> Yudisthira said, "Thou hast said what the duties are of the four modes of life and of the four orders [castes]. Tell me now, O grandsire, what are the principal duties of a kingdom."

> Bhishma said, "The (election and) coronation of a king is the first duty of a kingdom. A kingdom in which anarchy prevails becomes weak and is soon afflicted by robbers. In a kingdom torn by anarchy, righteousness [*dharma*] cannot dwell. The inhabitants devour one another. An anarchy is the worst possible of states. The *Shrutis* [Vedas] declare that in crowning a king, it is Indra that is crowned (in the person of the king). A person who is desirous of prosperity should worship the king as he should worship Indra himself. No one should dwell in kingdoms torn by anarchy. Agni does not convey (to the gods) the libations that are poured upon him in kingdoms where anarchy prevails. . . . They who live in countries where anarchy prevails cannot enjoy their wealth and wives. During times of anarchy, the sinful man derives great pleasure by robbing the wealth of other people. When, however, his (ill-got) wealth is snatched by others, he wishes for a king. It is evident, therefore, that in times of anarchy the very wicked even cannot be happy. The wealth of one is snatched away by two. That of the two is snatched away by many acting together. He who is not a slave is made a slave. Women, again, are forcibly abducted. For these reasons the gods created kings for protecting the people.

If there were no king on Earth for wielding the rod of chastisements, the strong would then have preyed on the weak. . . .

"In the absence of royal protection, all kinds of injustices would set in; an intermixture of castes would take place; and famine would ravage the kingdom. In consequence again of royal protection, men can everywhere sleep fearlessly at their ease without shutting their houses and doors with bolts and bars. Nobody would bear the evil speeches of others, far less actual assaults, if the king did not righteously protect the Earth. If the king exercises the duty of protection, women decked with every ornament may fearlessly wander everywhere without male relatives to attend upon them. Men become righteous and without injuring serve one another because the king exercises the duty of protection. In consequence of royal protection the members of the three orders [castes] are enabled to perform high sacrifices and devote themselves to the acquisition of learning with attention. The world depends upon agriculture and trade and is protected by the Vedas. All these again are duly protected by the king exercising his principal duty. Since the king, taking a heavy load upon himself protects his subjects with the aid of a mighty force, it is for this that the people are able to live in happiness. Who is there that will not worship him in whose existence the people exist and in whose destruction the people are destroyed? . . . No one should disregard the king by taking him for a man, for he is really a high divinity in human form."

The Ramayana

The second great epic of India is the Ramayana. Tradition says that the earliest version was the work of one man, the sage Valmiki. The story tells the adventures of Rama, who was unjustly exiled, and his wife, Sita. In popular Hinduism they are the supreme divine couple. Rama was an incarnation of the great sky god Vishnu. Sita, though understood to be an incarnation of Vishnu's wife, Laksmi, was represented as the daughter of the earth. Her adoptive father, King Janaka, found her as an infant when he was plowing a field. She was, in this way, born of the earth. To commemorate this, King Janaka named her Sita, meaning "furrow," the path a plow digs in the earth.

As Rama and Sita wandered through the forest of India, they passed through many places. These events did not become part of the main story. People from those areas compensated by elaborating on what happened when Rama was among them. So the Ramayana had many offshoots and regional and local variations that brought the main story to the local level without lessening its cosmic importance. Rama was god in human form, and he brought *dharma* (justice) wherever he went.

In the Ramayana, Rama and Sita enacted the ideal relationship between husband and

ई नही तेरेराजाजनकका बीजाराजा रांणामरबद्रीवांण
मामिञजी श्रीरांमचदजीनुकंहो धनयधेजायनेउचावो
नयधकंने जांयनेउन्नार्ह्या नेश्रीसितांजी सिएगार
जुनांबे ऊरोषांमेबवांहे तेरेश्रीमीतांजीकंहो मब्रते

ाय्ने मारोराजारियंजैनैजिसबद्करेबे

पांडीयो पिएधनय
उचावणेलोकगए
हे त्रीथधनयउयारने
वदावेताइएंगिरेगले
वरमालायालु म्श्री
यनुजीम्हारीमनबा
ुरमी सोश्रीरांमचं
दजीधनयककंनेत्रांय
नेउन्नार्हा तेरेराजा

This painting depicts a scene from the Ramayana in which Rama, shown at left, must break a bow in order to win the hand of Sita.

wife. Rama was god, while Sita was the ideal devotee who remained faithful to her god-husband no matter how unfair his actions may have seemed. She was the personification of the ideal Hindu wife, who is the source of her husband's prosperity because she bears his children—especially sons.

When Rama was exiled and about to leave home, he argued with Sita, who wanted to accompany him. In the course of this discussion, the obligations of a Hindu wife to her husband were made clear. When Sita found out that Rama had been exiled, she said: "My duty is clear, I shall dwell in the forest! For a woman, it is not her father, her son, nor her mother, friends nor her own self but the husband, who in this world and the next is ever her sole means of salvation. If thou enters the forest today, so shall I." Rama agreed to let her and his younger brother Laksmana accompany him. Laksmana personified the same manly virtues as Rama did and in addition displayed the proper deference and respect a younger brother should show to his elder brother.

Rama was the most perfect of princes and a great warrior, the embodiment of *dharma*. As a true *kshatriya*, he often battled demons who tried to interrupt the rituals of the brahmans. At the heart of the Ramayana, though, was the capture of Sita by the demon Ravana—who carried her off to Sri Lanka—and her eventual rescue by Rama. He accomplished the rescue with the help of the powerful and divine monkey king Hanuman and his monkey army, who built a bridge from India to Sri Lanka. Hanuman represented the ideal devotee and was known to always carry Rama and Sita within his heart.

The Dassehra Festival

The Dassehra festival—*dassehra* means "the tenth day"—is a ten-day enactment of the Ram Lila, another name for the Ramayana, during the time in September to October when the moon appears to grow larger in the sky. This festival is performed all over India. Late in the afternoon of the tenth day, on an outdoor stage, actors portray Ravana, Rama, Laksmana, and Hanuman. Ravana, the demon king, rises and swaggers around the stage. Hanuman rises to meet him, and they fight in a highly stylized manner. When Hanuman withdraws, Laksmana fights Ravana. Rama advances, and one of his attendants hands him a fire-arrow. As Rama releases his arrows, Ravana's banner catches fire and he falls to the ground. Hanuman, whose weapon is a club, beats Ravana, who dies as the sun sets amid cheers from the audience and the setting off of fireworks. The actors impersonating

A statue of the Hindu monkey god, Hanuman, stands outside the Kali Amman Temple in Singapore.

Rama, Laksmana, and Hanuman are taken in procession to the local Rama temple, where Rama will be worshipped.

Also on Dassehra, the Ramayana theme of the proper roles of husbands and wives is enacted by people in home rituals. A wife worships her husband, who takes on the part of Rama returning in triumph from his victory over Ravana. The wife draws a white square on the floor and places a wooden platform in its center. The husband stands on the platform while the wife washes his feet (a traditional gesture of hospitality), places a garland of flowers around his neck, and applies a *tilak* to his forehead. She then makes an offering of light (*arati*) to him by gently moving a small lamp before him as she would before a deity, presents him with offerings, and bows before him.

The Divali Festival

When Rama's period of exile was over, he, Sita, and Laksmana began the long journey home. Hindus celebrate Rama's return to his home city of Ayodhya every year at Divali, the Festival of Lights, during which lamps are lit on the three nights when there is a new moon. These are the darkest nights, making the lamps glow without competition from the moon. Divali has several related ceremonial events with many regional and caste-related variations. It takes place at the time of the autumnal equinox, which is the end of the rainy season, and it celebrates the return of the light and escape from the periods of decline and darkness. A central event of Divali is the performance of *puja* (worship), in this case directed to Laksmi, the goddess of wealth and prosperity and the wife of Vishnu.

During the Divali festival, in the Laksmi *puja*, Hindus place small lamps everywhere. They line rooftops, windowsills, and are placed all over the inside of house. It is believed that light attracts Laksmi.

puja

Puja, or worship of a deity, goes back to the sacrifice described in the Vedas, but it has been greatly simplified and can be performed alone, without a priest, at a small shrine or at home. The performance of public *puja*s can be traced to the rituals that were held in temples that began to be built in the fourth century in cities and in remote holy places that became stops along pilgrimage routes. These temples imitated the altars that were built for Vedic sacrifices, thus preserving continuity with the ancient forms of Hinduism. The Vedic sacrifices were burned in fires so that they could be conveyed to distant gods. In *puja*, whether performed in public or in private, the deity is believed to be present in his or her image or symbol, and offerings are made directly to that image. As *puja* became a widespread and popular form of religious practice, Vedic sacrifice also continued.

Hindu devotees worship the sun god on the banks of the Ganges River during the festival of Chatt Puja in the eastern Indian city of Patna. During the festival, Hindu women fast all day for the betterment of their family and society and take a dip in the holy river.

A Malaysian Hindu recites a prayer in front of oil lamps during Divali celebrations at a temple in Kota Bharu.

In villages, girls and young women sing religious songs as they walk to the well to decorate it with lamps. Firecrackers are set off for their light and to frighten away demons. —stored Groups of men may dance through the streets shouting out verses from the Ramayana. Altars are built to Laksmi on which are placed symbols of wealth: coins, ornaments, and cowrie shells (a kind of seashell). Some people place images of Krishna, Rama, Laksmana, Sita, and Hanuman on the altar, and many read or recite sections of the Ramayana. During *puja*, sweets and milk are offered to Laksmi. Such an offering transforms the sweets into *prasad*, sanctified food. That is, the worshipper gives food to the god or goddess, whose acceptance transforms it. What the god leaves uneaten is then the deity's gift to the devotee and is distributed among and consumed by the family members.

Divali is mainly about prosperity, which is enacted in various ways: many men gamble; merchants worship Laksmi as manifested in their account books and completely clean and repair their places of business; gifts are exchanged among family members and associations; houses are thoroughly cleaned and receive new coats of whitewash; and people take ritual baths. Everyone and everything that can be is made to look new and prosperous. The return of Rama and Sita was part of prosperity, for Rama then assumed the kingship and established the law of *dharma*. As a dharmic king, he assured the prosperity of the land, its animals, and its people.

four

Bhakti is a form of religious devotion introduced into Hinduism by the Bhagavad Gita, written sometime in the second or first century B.C.E. and popularized several centuries later through songs composed by Hindu saints. *Bhakti*, which means "passionate devotion," offers salvation to all because its only requirement is that one have the ability to feel love and devotion for god. It focuses attention on one god, most often Shiva or Krishna, as the great god who created all the other gods and everything and everyone else that exists. *Bhakti* differs from the Hinduism of the brahmans by offering salvation to everyone, regardless of caste, who experiences a wholehearted and passionate devotion to one god. Often this devotion is described as the emotions a woman experiences as she waits, longing for the return of her beloved. Such a love relationship between the devotee and the god is described in this poem by the Tamil (south Indian) writer and saint Appar, who lived in the seventh century.

> **Once she heard his name,**
> **then learned of his lovely form.**
> **Then she heard of his excellent town,**
> **and fell madly in love with him.**
> **That same day she left her mother and father**
> **and the proper ways of the world,**

lost herself,
lost her good name.
This woman has joined the feet
of the Lord, her lover.

An aspect of women's lives is revealed in this poem—women have more to lose in abandoning themselves to god. If they leave home to be with god, they lose their good reputation and can never get it back. The drama of this situation appealed to several other male poet-saints who also assumed female voices in their songs. Perhaps because of this emphasis on women's emotional experiences, several women themselves rose to prominence as poet-saints. Gradually *bhakti* movements spread all over south Asia, and in each region songs were composed in the local language, making the meaning accessible to all.

The Bhagavad Gita

The Bhagavad Gita is one of the world's great religious works and one of the most important texts of Hinduism. It is part of the Mahabharata. As the great civil war described in that epic is about to begin, Arjuna, the Pandava brother who is supposed to call both sides to war, has his chariot driven into the center of the battlefield, between the two opposing armies. There he raises a battle horn to his lips, but then hesitates. On both sides he sees relatives, friends, and men he respects, all of whom are about to kill each other. He is torn apart by despair, for he believes that to kill members of his family will destroy *dharma*. He throws down his bow and arrows.

The driver of his chariot is really Krishna, whom Arjuna knows only as a brave warrior, not as god in human form. Krishna calls Arjuna a coward and says that it is Arjuna's *dharma* as a warrior to fight. Arjuna answers that it would be better for him to become a renouncer than to kill those he should honor. Here is the central religious dilemma of the Bhagavad Gita: *dharma* is threatened by the war in which members of the same family will fight each other for the kingship, and *dharma* is threatened by Arjuna's refusal to fight. He is a *kshatriya*—a member of the warrior caste—and in the prime of his life, in the householder stage. He is too young to become a renouncer, therefore his *dharma* is to fight. To reconcile Arjuna to his duty, Krishna elaborates upon the teachings of the Upanishads and explains to Arjuna that the eternal self, the Atman, does not die and does not kill. The whole universe is Atman, and everyone has a spark of Atman within them. Only the body dies, the individual Atman returns to the universal Atman. Krishna says,

> **Know that that on which all this world is strung is imperishable: no one can bring about the destruction of this indestructible. What ends of this unending embodied, indestructible, and immeasurable being is just its bodies— therefore fight, Arjuna! He who thinks that this being is a killer and he who imagines that it is killed do neither of them know. Atman is not killed nor does it kill.**
>
> **It is never born nor does it die;**
> **Nor once that it is will it ever not be;**
> **Unborn, unending, eternal, and ancient**
> **It is not killed when the body is killed.**

Krishna continues to teach Arjuna. He explains that all action, whatever one does, causes karma, consequences that will shape the rest of one's life and all future lives. But, if one acts without attachment, no karma develops. This means that karma is caused by desiring a particular outcome to an action, by wanting to kill. However, if Arjuna acts with a mind disciplined by meditation, with detachment and without desire, there is no karma. Krishna is telling Arjuna that everything happens in and through god, not through human beings. One achieves detached actions through meditation, which leads to a higher understanding, an understanding that releases one from karma. Slowly, Krishna reveals that he is god and that the whole universe is contained in his divine form. He says,

> **When he sees me in everything and sees everything in me, I will not be lost to him and he will not be lost to me. He who shares in me as living in all creatures and thus becomes one with me, he is a yogi who, however he moves, moves in me. He is deemed the ultimate yogi, Arjuna, who, by comparing everything with himself, sees the same in everything, whether it be blissful or wretched.**

Yogis meditate and achieve this disciplined state of awareness; their minds are focused with devotion on Krishna and thus they always act through Krishna.

And the spiritual reality described by Krishna is open to everyone, rich or poor, of high or low caste. The value of the offering is not important, only the devotion with which it is given. Krishna explains *bhakti* and its consequences:

> **If one disciplined soul offers to me with love a leaf, a flower, fruit, or water, I accept this offering of love from him . . . and I shall undo the bonds of karma. . . . I am equable to all creatures, no one is hateful to me or dear—but those who share me with love are in me and I am in them. Even a hardened criminal who loves me and none other is to be**

deemed a saint, for he has the right conviction; he soon becomes law-minded and finds peace forever. Understand this, Arjuna: no servant of mine is lost. Even people of low origins, women, vaishyas, even shudras, go to the highest course if they rely on me. . . . May your thoughts be toward me, your love toward me, your sacrifice toward me, your homage toward me, and you shall come to me, having thus harnessed yourself to me as your highest goal.

Krishna is saying that devotion releases his devotees from reincarnation. When they die, they will join Krishna for all eternity.

shiva

As *bhakti* began to become a popular form of Hindu worship, Buddhism and Jainism continued to be active religions throughout India. In south India, however, in the seventh century there was a revival of the worship of Shiva at the same time that Hinduism began to assert itself over Buddhism and Jainism. So in south India those faiths gradually began to lose ground.

The Tamil poet and saint Appar of the seventh century had converted to Jainism and become a monk, but later when he became ill he prayed to Shiva, who cured him. Two of his poems that follow describe the worship of Shiva. When the first poem calls Shiva a madman, it refers to his wild nature as a wandering yogi.

Katavur Virattam's Lord [Shiva]
is like sweet sugar cane
to those who become the madman's devotees,
who rise at dawn to bathe, to gather fresh flowers,
and lovingly offer them in worship,
lighting lamps and burning incense for the rite.

shiva

Shiva is shown as a handsome ascetic, sitting in meditation, with four arms, one holding his symbol, a trident (a three-pronged spear). A cobra is wrapped around his neck, the crescent moon is in his hair, and the sacred Ganges River falls from heaven onto his head before descending to earth. Across his forehead three lines are drawn, which his followers sometimes draw across their own foreheads to increase their identification with the god and to be recognized as his devotees. In front of Shiva is a *lingam*, usually a black stone representing his creative power, that devotees worship by pouring milk over it and making offerings of flowers.

The second poem continues the description of Shiva and his worship. The second stanza refers to the practice of respectfully walking around the outside of a temple, called circumambulation, which is an important part of Hindu temple rituals.

Hands, join in worship,
strew fragrant flowers
on the Lord who binds
the hooded snake around his waist!
Hands, join in worship!

Of what use is the body
that never walked around the temple of Shiva,
offering him flowers in the worship rite?
Of what use is this body?

Another poem by Appar describes the feelings of Shiva's true followers, who know only joy because of their love for him.

> **I love him who dwells in the hearts of his lovers,**
> **whose great self is love itself.**
> **Desiring to see him, I melt;**
> **melting, I waste away.**
> **How shall my heart,**
> **[an] ant trapped on a two-headed firebrand,**
> **join my Father, the great Lord?**

krishna

From the fourteenth to the seventeenth centuries a devotional movement spread across northern and eastern India that believed Krishna to be the supreme god. In this tradition, Krishna was the playful lover, a simple cowherder to whom women—especially the *gopi*s, women who tended cows—were irresistibly drawn, especially when he played his flute. These young women abandoned their husbands, homes, and honor to be with Krishna. By giving up all that was valued in the everyday world, these women represented the ideal believer who, out of love for god, renounced everything else. Among the *gopi*s, Radha was greatly loved by Krishna. The following songs, which are taken from various Bengali collections, tell of their love. The erotic nature of the songs was intentional. Just as Radha demonstrated the deep longing one should feel toward god, Krishna, too, demonstrated his desire for union with his devotees.

> **Fingering the border of her friend's sari, [Radha was]**
> **nervous and afraid,**
> **sitting tensely on the edge of Krishna's couch,**
>
> **as her friend left she too looked to go**
> **but in desire Krishna blocked her way.**

This painting from the late seventeenth century pictures Krishna and Radha.

He was infatuated, she bewildered;
he was clever, and she naïve.

He put out his hand to touch her; she quickly pushed
it away.
He looked into her face, her eyes filled with tears.

He held her forcefully, she trembled violently
and hid her face from his kisses behind the edge of
her sari.

Then she lay down, frightened, beautiful as a doll;
he hovered like a bee round a lotus in a painting.

In the next poem Radha describes her feelings for Krishna.

As water to sea creatures,
moon nectar to chakora birds,
companionable dark to the stars—
my love is to Krishna.

My body hungers for his
as mirror image hungers
for twin of flesh.

His life cuts into my life
as the stain of the moon's rabbit
engraves the moon.

As if a day when no sun came up
and no color came to the earth—
that's how it is in my heart when he goes away.

The well-known Sri Meenakshi Temple in Madurai in south India.

These songs are usually sung in temples at the end of the day, with men sitting on one side of the temple and women on the other. Often a man keeps time on a drum while a second man plays a pair of small cymbals. By singing, the devotees hope to enter Radha's experience of the god and feel it themselves.

The next two songs describe the terrors Radha must overcome to find Krishna. Similarly, the devotee must leave the well-traveled path to find his or her own highly personal relationship with the divine.

O Madhava [Krishna], how shall I tell you of my terror?
I could not describe my coming here
if I had a million tongues.
When I left my room and saw the darkness
I trembled:
I could not see the path,
there were snakes that writhed round my ankles!

I was alone, a woman; the night was so dark,
the forest so dense and gloomy,
and I had so far to go.
The rain was pouring down—
which path should I take?
My feet were muddy
and burning where thorns had scratched them.
But I had the hope of seeing you, none of it mattered,
and now my terror seems far away. . . .
When the sound of your flute reaches my ears
it compels me to leave my home, my friends,
it draws me into the dark toward you.

The following song describes the pain of separation, the feeling of being cut off from god after one has known the bliss of union with him.

> **When they had made love**
> **she lay in his arms in the kunja grove.**
> **Suddenly she called his name**
> **and wept—as if she burned in the fire of separation.**
>
> **Where has he gone? Where has my love gone?**
> **O why has he left me alone?**
> **And she writhed on the ground in despair,**
> **only her pain kept her from fainting.**
> **Krishna was astonished**
> **and could not speak.**

In another song, Radha describes what she has given up in loving Krishna and yet how irresistible his call is.

> **The honey of his look, the radiance**
> **of his body—these**
> **were the bait and the snare he laid:**
> **and my eyes lit there like birds**
> **and at once were trapped,**
> **and my heart leapt like a doe into his nets**
> **leaving the cage of my breast empty,**
> **and goaded by his glance,**
> **my pride, that wild elephant,**
> **which I had kept**
> **chained night and day in my mind, broke loose**
> **and escaped me.**

At the first note of his flute
down came the lion gate of reverence for elders,
down came the door of dharma,
my guarded treasure of modesty was lost,
I was thrust to the ground as if by a thunderbolt.
Ah, yes, his dark body
poised in the tribanga (three curves) pose
shot the arrow that pierced me;
no more honor, my family
lost to me,
my home at Vraja
lost to me.
Only my life is left—and my life too
is only a breath that is leaving me.

An influential saint in the worship of Krishna was Chaitanya (1486–1534), who was born in Bengal. In his early twenties, he became mad with love for Krishna and devoted the rest of his life to him. Chaitanya became such a model follower that many other Krishna devotees were drawn to him, and Chaitanya became the leader of a flourishing religious group. Eventually his followers came to believe that he was simultaneously an incarnation of both Radha and Krishna. In 1514 he journeyed to Brindavan, near Mathura, which was believed to be the center of Krishna's activities when Krishna was incarnated as a cowherder. There, through meditation and trance, Chaitanya discovered sites and objects made sacred by the activities of Radha and Krishna. His disciples uncovered more places associated with Krishna's activities and so contributed a great deal to the path of Krishna pilgrimages in and around Brindavan. Unlike other *bhakti* saints, Chaitanya did not leave a legacy of songs but rather a legacy of visionary devotion expressed through ecstatic dancing and singing. He also originated the mantra of Krishna's names:

Hare Krishna Hare Krishna
Krishna Krishna Hare Hare
Hare Ram Hare Ram
Ram Ram Hare Hare.

Hare, sometimes spelled *Hari*, means "Lord." *Ram* is Rama, the hero of the Ramayana. Both Krishna and Rama are thought of as incarnations of Vishnu.

Mirabai (about 1500–1550) was one of the best known saints and composers of many songs about Krishna. She was born in Rajasthan, in northern India, and she thought of Krishna as her true husband. Consequently, her arranged marriage to an Indian prince was an unhappy one. Mirabai's devotion to Krishna and her associations with various religious followers so angered her husband's family that they tried to poison her. Eventually, she ran away to join a company of Krishna worshippers in Brindavan, by then the center of Krishna worship. She was rejected by the leading male saint of the time who refused to even speak with her because he had vowed never to speak to a woman. Mirabai made the point that there was only one man in Brindavan, Krishna, because all true devotees are female in relation to god.

To this day, *bhakta*s, people who practice *bhakti*, cultivate a highly personal relationship with their god in which they often concentrate on one of his qualities. In Mirabai's case, her poems frequently emphasize Krishna's dark skin and his feat of having once lifted a mountain to protect his followers. Often she called him *hari*, lord. In the following poem, *rana* may refer either to her father-in-law or her husband, and she calls herself Mira.

Life without Hari is no life, friend,
And though my mother-in-law fights,
my sister-in-law teases,
the rana is angered,

A guard is stationed on a stool outside,
and a lock is mounted on the door,
How can I abandon the love I have loved
in life after life?

Mira's Lord is the clever Mountain Lifter:
Why would I want anyone else?

soon after the introduction of *bhakti* or devotion to one god, new, powerful, and fierce goddesses (*devi*s) began to emerge. This arose from village culture and from the many tribal peoples of India. Gradually, some of these goddesses were incorporated into the brahmanical tradition, and some of the previously minor Vedic goddesses became more important. These goddesses all share the name Mahadevi (Great Goddess), which includes different forms of one active, powerful creator. She is often simply called Ma or Amma (mother). She created the universe, and she will destroy it. Until then she maintains the world both in her peaceful and her fierce forms. In present-day rural India, this dual nature of the Goddess is expressed through the belief that the local village goddesses, depending on their moods, can bring either fertility or plague. Despite these awesome powers, the Goddess is perceived by her devotees as present and responsive to their needs; she protects them from harm and grants blessings. Even better, she can grant wisdom and liberation. Often she is called Mahamaya (Great Illusion). This indicates her powers and the veil of illusion she has spread over the world that prevents people from attaining liberation, but which can be pierced by her grace and by practicing meditation.

Durga

One story about the Goddess in her fierce form is that of Durga slaying the buffalo demon, Mahisa. It is described in *The Devimahatmya* (*The*

A thirteenth-century painting from Rajasthan in north India shows the goddess Durga vanquishing the buffalo demon Mahisa.

Glorification of the Goddess), a text included in *The Markandeya Purana* that was collected between 400 and 600 C.E. It describes Durga's creation from the energies of various male gods in order to fight a fierce buffalo demon who could be destroyed only by a female. Once born, however, she was uncontrollable, and did as she pleased, honoring no one and no god. She refused to marry and so remained an independent being, unlike all the married goddesses who were subject to the wills of their husbands. Despite this description, she is often spoken of as being the wife of Shiva, or of being his *shakti*, the source of his power.

As the following account of the battle shows, Durga, who is called Candika and Ambika (Mother) in this story, is a ferocious warrior.

> The demon Mahisa himself, in the form of a buffalo, terrorized the troops of the goddess. Some of them he beat with his snout, others he trampled with his hooves, still others he lashed with his tail, while some were ripped to shreds by his horns. . . . After felling her troops, the demon rushed to attack the lion that was with the great goddess. . . .
>
> When she saw the great demon attacking, swelling with rage, Candika then became furious enough to destroy him. She threw her noose and lassoed the great demon. Thus trapped in that mighty battle, he abandoned his buffalo shape and became a lion. At the moment Ambika cut off its head, a man appeared, sword in hand. As soon as Ambika cut down that man along with his sword and shield, the demon became a huge elephant. With a roar he dragged the goddess's lion along with his trunk, but while he was pulling the lion, she cut off his trunk with her sword. Then the great demon resumed his wondrous

buffalo shape, causing all three worlds with the moving and unmoving creatures to tremble. . . . The goddess flew up and trod on his throat with her foot, piercing him with her spear. Crushed by her foot, overcome by the power of that goddess, the demon came half-way out of his own mouth. Still battling in this way, he was felled by the goddess who cut off his head with her mighty sword. So that demon Mahisa, his army and his allies, who had so distressed the three worlds, were all annihilated by the goddess.

The battle between various demons and the gods, or between the forces of good and evil, is a continuing theme in Hinduism.

Kali

The Devimahatmya also describes the creation of the goddess Kali. In the following excerpt, during the heat of battle, Durga, again called Ambika (Mother), gives birth to Kali. In this battle the demons

saw the goddess, smiling slightly, positioned on her lion atop the great golden peak of a mighty mountain. When they saw her, they made zealous efforts to seize her, while other demons from the battle approached her with bows and swords drawn. Then Ambika became violently angry with her enemies, her face growing black as ink with rage. Suddenly there issued forth from between her eyebrows Kali, with protruding fangs, carrying a sword and a noose, with a mottled, skull-topped staff, adorned with a necklace of human skulls, covered with a tiger-skin, gruesome with shriveled flesh. Her mouth gaping wide, her lolling tongue terrifying, her eyes red and sunken, she filled the whole of space with her howling. Attacking and killing the mighty demons, she devoured the armed force of the enemies of the gods. Seizing with one hand the elephants with their back-riders, drivers, warriors and bells, she hurled them into her mouth. In the same way she chewed up warriors with their horses, chariots and charioteers, grinding them up most horribly with her teeth. One she grabbed by the hair of the head, another by the nape of the neck, another she trod underfoot while another she crushed against her chest. The mighty striking and throwing weapons loosed by those demons she caught in her mouth and pulverized in fury. She ravaged the entire army of powerful evil-souled demons; some she devoured while others she trampled; some were slain by the sword, others bashed by her skull-topped club, while other demons went to perdition crushed by the sharp points of her teeth. . . . Then howling horribly, Kali laughed aloud malevolently, her mouth gaping wide, her fangs glittering, awful to behold. Astride her huge lion, the goddess rushed against [the demon named] Canda; grabbing his head by the hair, she decapitated him with her sword. When he saw Canda dead [the demon called] Munda attacked, but she threw him too to the ground, stabbing him with her sword in rage. See both Canda and the mighty Munda felled, the remains of the army fled in all directions, overcome with fear. . . .

In such a way, then, does the divine goddess, although eternal, take birth again and again to protect creation. This world is deluded by her; it is begotten by her; it is she who gives knowledge when prayed to and prosperity when pleased. By Mahakali (Great Kali) is this entire egg of Brahma pervaded. At the awful time of dissolution she takes on the form of Mahamari, the great destructress of the world. She is also its unborn source; eternal, she sustains creatures in time. As Laksmi, or Good Fortune, she bestows wealth on men's homes in times of prosperity. In times of disaster she appears as Misfortune for their annihilation. When the goddess is praised and worshipped with flowers, incense, perfume and other gifts, she gives wealth, sons, a mind set upon *Dharma*, and happiness to all mankind.

This eighteenth-century manuscript painting shows the goddess Kali dancing on the corpse of one of her victims.

Indian goddesses can be divided into two groups. Belonging to the first group are the goddesses who are married and have essentially benevolent natures because they are believed to be "tamed" by their husbands. Belonging to the second group are the goddesses who are unmarried, and therefore untamed, deities with fierce natures like Durga and Kali, who demand blood sacrifices. An important part of worshipping fierce goddesses is the sacrifice of animals. Temples served by brahmans, who are vegetarian, get around this requirement by "using symbolic substitutes for meat (red flowers, red cloth, the cutting of a cucumber or gourd instead of a goat) or by insisting that actual animal sacrifice be conducted by low-caste menials outside the temple." Though Kali receives animal sacrifices, she is also widely worshipped in her gentle form, as the benevolent mother who gives blessings to her followers and who accepts offerings of flowers and incense.

The Navaratri festival

Navaratri, meaning "nine nights," is the great autumnal festival of the goddess that takes place following the new moon that happens at the end of September or the start of October. It is celebrated throughout the Hindu world to welcome prosperity at the end of the rainy season. Called Durgotsava or Durga Puja, it commemorates Durga's battle with the buffalo demon Mahisa, which is said to have lasted nine days, the length of her festival. This battle restored order to the world, enabling people to prosper. The actual or symbolic sacrifice of an animal is particularly important to Durga Puja because the battle it recalls ends with her killing an animal demon. Yet in this festival Durga is also understood to be the goddess who makes everything grow. In most parts of India, this is shown by representing her with nine bundles of different plants and with a pot in which grain has been put that will sprout during the festival. Local goddesses can, however, take Durga's place as the center of the festival.

In Nepal, on the first day of the festival, a Durga altar is erected in a locked, darkened room into which only the initiated men of the family

These women wear red powder on their faces to honor Durga. They pray as they celebrate the final day of the Durga Puja in Dkaha, Bangladesh.

may go. During this time the women of the household may not enter this room. Each morning of the festival, the male head of the household bathes and then goes to the Durga temple and returns with offerings for his family. He then worships Durga in the family's altar room. Again, in the evening, he worships her with lighted lamps. On the eighth day, a black male goat is sacrificed, and on the tenth day the family shrine room is opened to women and children. This male dominance of Durga's festival is balanced by the female dominance of Parvati's festival. Anthropologist Lynn Bennett has suggested that Durga presents such a fearful aspect of womanhood to men that they must ritually control and subdue her. Meanwhile, many women feel closer to Parvati because, like themselves, she is married and she has problems similar to their own.

parvati

Parvati is a married goddess of great complexity. While always the obedient and faithful wife of the god Shiva, the stories surrounding her describe an independent and willful individual. Parvati breaks the tradition of having her parents choose her husband when she sets her mind on Shiva and seeks his favor not through feminine wiles, but through ascetic practices. The following excerpt from *The Siva Satarudriya Purana* tells of Shiva's testing Parvati's ascetic practices (*tapas*).

> He saw the goddess standing at a fire altar surrounded by her companions, pure like an auspicious digit of the moon. When Shiva . . . saw the goddess, he approached her eagerly in a friendly manner. When she saw him coming, [disguised] as an aged ascetic with matted hair carrying a water jar, she worshipped him most graciously with all the offerings of a *puja*. . . . Parvati inquired respectfully about his health, [and asked who he was].
>
> "I am an ascetic, going where I please, a benefactor who gives help to others."
>
> "A great perversion is going on here, I see conduct that will bring disaster. For in your early youth when you should be enjoying fine pleasures and the attentions of others, you are doing *tapas* to no purpose at all. Why are you practicing *tapas* in this lonely forest, *tapas* that is hard to master even for self-controlled seers?"
>
> [Parvati answered:] "I realize my purpose is most difficult to obtain. How am I to succeed? In any case, it is because of my heart's desire that I am now practicing *tapas*. Disregarding all the other gods who are headed by

Indra, leaving aside even Vishnu and Brahma, I want in truth to win for my husband only Shiva."

[Continuing his disguise, Shiva heaps insults on Shiva, who Parvati defends, and then Shiva reveals himself.]

Assuming his divine form as its appears to those who meditate on him, Shiva made himself visible and spoke to her.

"I will not leave you alone. I have tested you, blameless woman, and find you firmly devoted to me. I came to you in the form of an ascetic and said to you many things, all out of desire for your own welfare. I am profoundly pleased with your special devotion. Tell me what your heart desires! There is nothing you do not deserve! Because of your *tapas*, I shall be your servant from this moment on. Due to your loveliness, each instant without you lasts an Age. Cast off your modesty! Become my wife forevermore! Come, beloved. I shall to my mountain at once, together with you.

SIX

Around the same time as powerful goddesses began to emerge, so too did Tantric forms of Hinduism (around the fourth to sixth centuries C.E.). Tantra has its roots in ancient and non-brahmanical religious beliefs such as the worship of fierce goddesses, magical practices, and shamanism. Shamanism involves ecstatic ritual journeys (trances) in which the shaman, a religious expert, is supposed to meet and overcome gods and demons to gain their powers. Tantra recognizes many terrifying deities whose powers are sought by devotees. Among these deities are the god Shiva, in the form of Bhairava, accompanied by frightening female deities known as *dakini*s and *yogini*s and the Goddess in her fierce form. Yoga, meditation, and ascetic practices were also incorporated into Tantra, which spread throughout the Hindu world as well as the Buddhist and Jain worlds.

Tantra stresses achieving enlightenment in one lifetime through extreme practices involving individual visionary experiences, vivid sexual imagery, and the use of forbidden substances like wine and meat in its rituals. Tantrikas, or people who practice Tantra, use desire to seek liberation; they do not reject the world, but instead they use the things of the world, including their own bodies. Tantrikas are free of the world and desire because they have realized the Ultimate Reality. Tantric practices often take place at night and in cemeteries to avoid the prying eyes of the non-initiated and to conquer the fear of death. Otherwise Tantric rituals are performed in private by small groups. Tantra's ideal type is the *siddha* (from the word *siddhi*, meaning "someone with supernatural powers") or *sadhu* (holy man), a wandering yogi who also works wonders. The behavior of *siddhas* and *sadhus* is often designed to shock people and to break the social taboos that Tantrikas believe keep people from seeing Ultimate Reality, a realm in which there is no right or wrong. There were and are women Tantrikas, but most often the tradition concerns men and male experience.

Tantric practices were gradually subdued and incorporated into mainstream Hindu practice. Many brahmans became members of Tantric sects and dedicated written works to Tantra, such as Abhinavagupta (tenth century). The *siddha* tradition, however, continues to flourish among individual wandering yogis. The influence of Tantra is pervasive in modern Hinduism as seen in *puja*, art, and deities, yet the majority of Hindus do not regard themselves as Tantrikas.

One of the unique elements of Tantric ritual are the "five *m*'s": wine, meat, fish, toasted grain, and sexual union (words that in Sanskrit all begin with the letter *m*). The first four are described as substances that stimulate desire. They lead up to the fifth—actual or symbolic sexual union. There are two forms of practice: the right-handed path, which uses substitutes for the first four and visualizes the fifth (sexual union); and the left-handed path, in which the first four things are drunk or eaten and sexual intercourse is ritualized.

The five *m*'s are forbidden to Hindus because they are polluting, but the Tantric practitioner ritually uses these forbidden substances to get beyond the concepts of good and evil, forbidden and allowed, and to achieve an experience of the ultimate union of all opposites, even of female and male. In Tantra, reality is one, but in ordinary life it is often made up of dualities. Tantra utilizes the concept of duality to achieve enlightenment. It emphasizes a supreme deity that is female

A *sadhu*, or holy man, worships Shiva on the banks of the Ganges
River.

and male and whose divine power is present throughout the universe and in each individual. For example, those who worship Shiva and the goddess known as Shakti think of Shiva as passive intelligence and Shakti as active primal matter. From their union everything else in the universe arises, yet they are really one. Through visualization practices during rituals or meditation, worshippers seek to merge with the gods and their *shakti*s, meaning "power" or "energy" and referring to the goddesses who are their wives. They believe that the union of Shiva and Shakti can take place right here and right now, in the world at large, as well as within one's own body. Tantric sexual practices repeat "at a human level the activity of the divine couple, whose creative bliss is echoed and possibly even reproduced by the human pair." By emphasizing the role of the human body in salvation, Tantra stresses the essential divinity of humanity. Divine power is within each person, and Tantric practices attempt to draw on or awaken this power in order to achieve liberation.

In Tantra and other Hindu traditions, human beings are said to be composed of three elements: the physical body, the subtle body (an imagined body), and the eternal self or spirit (Atman) that is part of the divine. *Cakra*s (meaning "wheels" or "circles") are mystical points or centers in the subtle body, and although they can be experienced during meditation, they have no actual physical reality. They are both symbols for and stages of spiritual experience that are perceived in physical, mental, and cosmic terms.

Five or seven *cakra*s, depending on the system, are aligned along the spine of the subtle body. Each *cakra* is associated with a specific color, shape, sound, animal, and deity. A Tantrika first activates the *cakra* at the base of the spine and then draws that energy up the

This Sri Lankan painting portrays the seven *cakra*s, the mystical centers of the human body.

spine, activating each *cakra* in turn. Activation is brought about by awakening the kundalini, envisioned as a female serpent lying coiled and sleeping around the first *cakra*. This is accomplished through forms of meditation and body postures, especially those that teach breath control and thus control energy or the life force of the subtle body. Kundalini is the energy (*shakti*) that enlivens each *cakra* in order to awaken its powers for the yogi. While in meditation, the Tantrika visualizes the *cakra*s and the gods within them, achieving a spiritual union with each deity, one by one, moving up the spine. Success in this practice leads to greater and greater states of consciousness and ends in liberation.

The system of *cakra*s and the subtle body are important in Tantric practices that emphasize the physical body as the means to achieve liberation. Although the body—with its fears and desires—can limit spiritual advancement, by rightly understanding the body in all its complexity, the believer can transform it into a vehicle for liberation. What was a limitation, when properly tuned by activating the *cakra*s, becomes the means to freedom. As the kundalini rises through each *cakra*, it awakens that *cakra*, which raises the practitioner's consciousness. When the kundalini reaches the highest *cakra* at the top of the head, the perception of all dualities falls away; there is only the divine oneness.

Underlying this system is the belief that humans are the measure of the universe, that the human body reflects and contains spiritual truths.

There are three main Tantric sects. One (Vaishnavas) worships Vishnu in the form of Krishna as the supreme deity; another (Shaivas) worships Shiva; and another (Shaktas) worships the Goddess. The last two are sometimes hard to distinguish because they are perceived as being inseparable. Tantric texts reflect these sectarian differences. Yet, in all the sects, it is *shakti* (energy) that "produces, pervades, sustains, and finally reabsorbs the universe."

Esoteric Tantric texts and practices are purposely difficult to understand because these teachings are supposed to be kept secret. They require complete dependence on a guru, a spiritual teacher, for preliminary training followed by initiation. Without initiation and instruction, the texts remain obscure and the rituals unknowable. Tantric rituals are believed to contact powerful and dangerous forces, so the initiate must be confident that he or she has been instructed by someone with an even more powerful divine source. Typically, the guru secretly gives the initiate a mantra: syllables and Sanskrit words that are believed to embody a deity's power and, when they are uttered, grant power over various other deities. Mantras are also used to invoke deities. Since visualization is also an important part of Tantric practice, there is a rich legacy of Tantric art. The art includes the geometrical designs of mandalas, which means "circle," and *yantras*, which means "support," that are used for rituals, meditation, and visualizations. The basic form of a mandala is a circle enclosed in a square that is enclosed in an outer circle.

Mandalas

Mandalas are designed to represent the whole of reality and are an important part of Tantric initiation rituals. They can be either temporary or more lasting works of art. Temporary mandalas are constructed on ground that has been purified and over which a pavilion has been erected. The drawing or laying out of the mandala is the first step in rituals that invite various supernatural beings and powers to take up residence in it. During the initiation ceremony, the initiate symbolically enters the mandala, sometimes by tossing a flower into it. She or he assumes the powers of the deities located in it by envisioning all its details and reciting mantras accompanied by ritual hand gestures (mudras) that express religious concepts. In this way the body, mind, and speech of the initiate are fully engaged respectively by their gestures, visualizations, and repetitions of the mantras. Her or his sense of personal individuality is put aside to break down the concept of duality. Within the mandala there is only the complete union of initiate and deity. At the end of the ritual, mandalas are respectfully taken apart and disposed of in a river.

There are detailed textual descriptions of mandalas to help the Tantrika visualize all its aspects, describing its central deity and the many other deities that guard its different sections. Paintings and sculptures also support personal visualization practices. They help the meditator accurately visualize every detail of the deity, such as the objects the deity holds, which define his or her powers.

Yantras

Yantras are abstract and dynamic representations of the deities and their powers. Often the outward movement of the drawing depicts creation and its inward movement the absorption of the universe. The creation and absorption of the universe are represented by the union of female and male, as in the famous Shricakra Yantra. Shri is the goddess or Shakti. Triangles emanate from its center, enclosed in circles of lotus petals (symbols of divinity), which in turn are enclosed in a square with four doors opening toward north, south, east, and west. The upward-pointing triangles represent Shiva; the downward-pointing ones represent Shakti. A devotee meditates on the *yantra* while reciting mantras to evoke the powers of the deities.

The use of mantras goes back to the Vedic hymns that were used to praise the gods and gain their aid. They continue to be used throughout the Hindu world, not just among Tantric practitioners. A mantra can be as simple as repeatedly saying the god's name, such as "Hari, Hari Krishna," with *hari* meaning "Lord." Hindus believe that every deity has two forms: their image, which can be seen in abstract or realistic works of art; and their sound form, which can be heard in mantras. The god is present in all these forms, which are part of meditations or rituals that call forth the god or goddess and his or her powers.

Important Tantric pilgrimage sites are connected to a well-known legend in which Shakti and Shiva were married. She was called Sati and he, Rudra. When Sati's father insulted Sati's husband by not inviting him to a sacrifice, she killed herself. Shiva was inconsolable at her death and he danced wildly all over the earth while carrying her body on his shoulders. Gradually, parts of her body fell off. The places that they landed became *pitha*s, pilgrimage sites of the Goddess.

From about the eighth to the fourteenth centuries Tantra flourished in India and Nepal, spreading as far as Cambodia and Indonesia. This can be seen in the many texts and artistic creations, such as the temples of central India that date from this period, the best known being Khajuraho.

Hinduism is rich in diverse religious practices that have developed over time, but it has always remained faithful to the religious authority of the Vedas and the Upanishads. Although it has incorporated village traditions, such as local goddesses, and a variety of ascetic practices, such as yoga, meditation, and isolation from society, examples of these are also found in the Vedas and Upanishads.

One can understand Hindu worship by recognizing two types of divinities: pure and impure. Pure divinities are the great gods Vishnu and Shiva and their incarnations, such as Rama and Krishna. The Great Goddess is sometimes, but not always, included among pure divinities. In their temples pure divinities are offered pure vegetarian food by brahman priests. In recent years the Indian government has legislated that all castes have access to these temples; in the past, the low castes were excluded. The low castes, however, also maintain their own temples, where impure, mostly regional goddesses and gods are served non-vegetarian offerings in the form of sacrifices of male goats, roosters, and sometimes water buffalo.

seven

FOREIGN RULE AND THE HINDU RENAISSANCE

While Hinduism was flourishing, Turko-Afghan invaders began entering northwestern India in the eleventh century. At first these were just raids to plunder India's riches, but eventually they came to stay. These Muslim warriors were a tremendous threat to Hinduism, because the Muslim faith opposes idolatry—worshipping of a physical object as a god—and a large part of Hinduism focuses on worshipping gods through images. On their raids of India, Muslim troops smashed statues of Hindu gods and destroyed temples, carrying off their treasures. Their destruction of Buddhist monasteries, temples, and universities was so complete that the Buddhist faith largely died out in India. India, however, had met invaders before, going back at least to Alexander the Great (356–323 B.C.E.), and it tended to have two reactions to such invasions: to absorb the invaders within the Hindu social order by defining them as a new caste and by reaffirming Hindu orthodoxy in the face of foreign religious beliefs.

Politically, especially in the north and centered on Delhi, India was ruled by Muslims (the Delhi sultanate, 1206–1526), who were for the most part content to let local Hindu ruling families act as local governors, provided they sent tribute to Delhi and supplied men for its armies. Outside India the Mongols were moving westward into the Muslim world, spreading terror and destruction. For safety, many Muslims fled to India, bringing their faith, culture, language, and arts with them. Muslim influence on and conquest of other areas of India was slow, but persistent. Hindu princes, however, fought back. If the battle seemed hopeless or to show their determination and courage, some Hindu soldiers rode into battle dressed in the orange robes and turbans of renouncers, signifying that even though they were householders, they were now at the end of their lives. They would die in battle, fulfilling their *dharma* as warriors and having completed the four stages of life. The Indian resistance to Muslim rule was the beginning of the idea of Hindu nationalism, an idea that had its roots in the epics' emphasis on the importance of dharmic kings.

During the three centuries of Muslim rule, a regional Hindu ruler was sometimes able to overthrow a sultan's control, and contending armies marched back and forth all over India. It was a time of unrest and danger. New restrictions were placed on Hindu women. In the past, high caste women had covered their hair and remained mainly in their homes. This practice then solidified into *purdah*, the Muslim practice of totally veiling women's faces and keeping them in seclusion. Caste rules were also more strictly enforced as high caste Hindu men struggled to keep their society from changing.

Out of the popular *bhakti* movements that continued to spread across India, two holy men—Kabir (about 1440–1518) of Benares and Guru Nanak (1469–1539) of the Punjab—preached devotion to one god that combined Hindu *bhakti* with Sufism, the mystical form of Islam that also sought union with god.

Actually, Sufism, which like *bhakti*, emphasized a direct experience of god, was quite influential in the spread of Islam in India. Hinduism had a long tradition of singling out one god for worship, and some Hindus felt comfortable with the monotheism of Islam. The Sufis were influenced by the passionate devotion of the Hindu poet-saints.

Both Kabir and Nanak believed they were restoring true Hinduism which had become corrupted and superstitious. They rejected the caste system and the external trappings of Hinduism, such as idol worship, fasts, and pilgrimages. In their places, one should only continually sing praises of god and try to experience his grace and love. Even though Kabir and Nanak had a profound influence on religious life in northern India, many orthodox Hindus and Muslims denounced them.

To the south, on India's western coast, the Portuguese explorer Vasco da Gama sailed into the port of Calicut in 1498, beginning an era of gradual European penetration and conquest that would last until Indian independence in 1947. There were fortunes to be made in selling Indian spices in Europe. Along with soldiers and traders, Catholic missionaries were sent to India, and they began to gain converts in the mostly Hindu population. The English were not far behind the Portuguese, and they formed a trade agreement with Emperor Jahangir (who ruled 1605–1627).

Muslim rule solidified under the Mughal empire (1526–1764), especially under Emperor Akbar (who ruled 1556–1605), an enlightened and religiously tolerant leader. Unfortunately, many of his policies were abandoned by his successors, particularly Emperor Aurangzeb (who ruled 1658–1707), who placed restrictions on Hindu practices and heavily increased taxes of Hindus. During his harsh reign, there were many rebellions led by Hindus and Sikhs, followers of Guru Nanak.

A Hindu resistance movement also arose under Shahji of Maharashtra, his son Shivaji (1627–680), and other regional groups. All these groups used guerrilla warfare to keep the Mughal army away, though they could never unite among themselves. After the death of Aurangzeb in 1707, warring factions within the Mughal court, foreign invasions in the northwest, and an army divided to fight various rebellions undermined the Mughal empire. Europeans, especially the English and the French, were poised on the coasts of India in trading centers, ready to seize control of a country in such disorder. A series of incidents and a few battles left the English in charge. Instead of trying to rule India, they decided to offer their "services" to the crumbling empire and to smaller local rulers in exchange for revenues from large

A Sikh prays inside the holy pond of the Golden Temple in the northern Indian city of Amritsar. The Golden Temple is the Sikhs' most sacred site.

sikhs

Sikhs were and are mainly people of the Punjab of northwestern India. They are followers of a religion founded by Guru Nanak who taught a path of devotion to one god that blended Hindu *bhakti* with Sufi mysticism. Sikhs are monotheistic and believe in karma and reincarnation. They oppose the caste system and renunciation, and in the sixteenth century they abolished the *purdah*, the seclusion of women. They did not get along well with the Muslim rulers in Delhi. Emperor Jahangir charged their leader, Guru Arjun (1563–1606), with treason and tortured him to death. This act turned the originally peaceful Sikhs into a military group united against Mughal tyranny. Then Emperor Aurangzeb arrested another Sikh guru and had him beheaded for refusing to convert to Islam. After this, Sikhs took on what became the five symbols of their faith: never to cut their hair or beards, always to carry a sword, to wear a steel bracelet on their right wrists, to wear knee-length soldier's shorts, and to keep a comb for their hair.

parts of India. By the end of the eighteenth century, the English wanted to trade, to make money, and not to rule India. This would gradually change over the course of the next century as England, through its trading office—the East India Company—acquired more territory and greater control over regional rulers, and more young Englishmen came to India to make their fortunes.

As hardheaded businessmen with their eyes firmly fixed on profit, the English initially opposed the arrival of Christian missionaries who, by converting the Indians, would stir up unrest that would not be good for business. It was not until 1813 that missionaries were allowed free access to India. Some of these were men of intelligence who worked hard to learn the local languages and to study India's culture. Others were zealots who trampled on local religious feelings and generated hostility toward the English.

As the land owned by the East India Company continued to grow, it required more administrators. The English decided it would be useful to teach Indians English and give them a basic Western education so that they could work for the East India Company. The missionaries proved able teachers, and they set up schools that also spread their ideas about Christianity.

English Rule and the Hindu Renaissance

The creation of schools and jobs among the English led to new opportunities for wealth, power, and prestige among those Indians who could bridge the gap between their own culture and British colonial society. It also created a new elite class of Indians who gradually became alienated from their own culture due to their immersion in the English educational system and the English work situation.

Most of the East India Company's activity centered in Calcutta, in the state of Bengal, and it was here that a synthesis of Anglo-Indian (English and Indian) culture began to emerge that would shape Indian nationalism, though the Punjab and Maharastra regions of India were also significant contributors in the creation of a new Hindu consciousness. Part of this new way of thinking was a reaction against Western values and a reassertion of Hindu values and traditions. This marks the beginning of the Hindu Renaissance, the reinterpretation of Hindu culture and belief in light of Christian criticism, which was along the same lines as that of the Muslims: it was polytheistic, and Hindus were idolaters. In responding to this spiritual and intellectual onslaught, Hindus maintained their essential ideas and values, while drawing on useful Western social and political concepts.

In the nineteenth century, three groups influenced the future of Hinduism: reformers, mystics, and Westerners. All three thought that the ancient religious texts of India remained relevant to what they thought was the need of the time: the reformation of Hinduism and Hindu society. Social reformers particularly focused on Hindu women. They advocated ending child marriage and *sati* (the practice of widows sacrificing themselves on the funeral mounds of their deceased husbands) and promoted the education of women.

Ram Mohun Roy

Known as the father of the Hindu Renaissance, Ram Mohun Roy (1772–1833) was a Bengali brahman who, in his youth, worked for the East India Company. When challenged by Christian missionaries, he studied the ancient texts of Hinduism, especially the Upanishads, which led him to found the Brahmo Samaj (Society of Brahma). This organization was to have an enormous effect on Hindu cultural life and religious belief and continues to be an influential religious force in India. Roy reinterpreted Hinduism by focusing on the monistic (belief in one divine principle) ideas of the Upanishads as expressed in the relationship of Atman and Brahman. In this way he challenged Christian charges that Hinduism was a polytheistic religion. Roy also rejected idolatry, sacrifice, reincarnation, and karma, along with the caste system and *sati*. He did, however, copy some of the patterns of organization used by the Christian Church which helped his movement to flourish throughout India, and he acknowledged that truth existed in all religions. While holding on to some Hindu ideas and to Indian culture, Roy embraced Western ways.

swami Dayananda sarasvati

In 1875 a wandering Hindu holy man from Gujarat, Swami Dayananda Sarasvati (1824–1883), responded to the challenges of Christianity in Bombay, now called Mumbai. He founded Arya Samaj (Society of Aryan Believers), an organization that was to have its greatest success in the Punjab. In contrast to Roy, Sarasvati rejected Western values and was critical of Christianity and Islam. He emphasized the Vedas, claiming that they were completely monotheistic and that they contained all truth, even modern scientific ideas. He dismissed the idea that Hinduism was a polytheistic religion by claiming that all the Hindu gods were attributes of one universal god. He rejected contemporary forms of Hinduism as corrupt because they did not follow the Vedas. In particular, he claimed that the Vedas did not approve of child marriage. By examining the Vedas, Hindus could answer their Christian critics from within their own tradition. Members of Arya Samaj moved into villages, where they created a network of schools and colleges that challenged the control of Western-style education.

Ramakrishna

Mystics of the Hindu Renaissance are associated with Sri Ramakrishna (1834–1886), a man who had no actual concern with either social or political reform, but who nevertheless was widely influential in India and abroad. Ramakrishna led a deeply mystical life strongly influenced by *bhakti* and Tantra. He claimed to have personally experienced the oneness of god through his visions of Kali, Jesus, Buddha, and Allah (the God of Islam), though he was especially devoted to the goddess Kali. His life was proof of the relevance of the Hindu saint in modern India. He drew thousands of followers but his main disciple and spiritual heir was Vivekananda (1863–1902), who brought Ramakrishna's message to the West and popularized the idea that the West must learn from Indian spirituality.

In 1893 the World Parliament of Religions, an extraordinary meeting of representatives from almost all the world's great religions, was held in Chicago. Extensively covered by the American press, this meeting introduced many forms of world religion to Americans. Vivekananda appeared as the last speaker. He made a deep impression on those who heard him and went on to give many lectures throughout the United States during his three-year stay. His enthusiasm for Western converts to Hinduism led him to establish the Vedanta Society in New York City in 1896, an organization that today has branches throughout the United States. He popularized this society through his lectures and writings. He returned to India as a hero of Hindu self-pride. He organized the pan-Indian Ramakrishna Mission to spread his and Ramakrisna's teachings and to relieve physical poverty. Today the organization has many branches in India. Vivekanada argued that although India could learn from the technology of the West, "the West must learn to drink from the fountain of Indian spirituality." He was the first guru to become prominent in India because of the popularity he had gained in the West.

The Theosophical Society

The third group to influence Hinduism was initially made up of Westerners who were members of the Theosophical Society. This was the first time Indians heard Hinduism praised by Westerners as being superior to Christianity.

In the late nineteenth century, many Westerners were attracted to the religions of Asia. In 1889 two prominent Westerners journeyed to

Mohandas Gandhi, in a photograph taken in the 1940s.

colonial Sri Lanka and publicly converted to Buddhism. They were Helena Petrovna Blavatsky and Henry Steel Olcott, founders of the Theosophical Society. Its goals include the study of ancient world religions in order to draw a universal ethical code from them. Through the influence of its members and its many publications, it revitalized both Hinduism and Buddhism in India and popularized them in the West by presenting them in ways that would be acceptable to Westerners. The Theosophical Society remains an important tradition in south Asia, though it has declined in the West.

These three movements of reformers, mystics, and Westerners had an enormous effect on an influential and powerful section of the Indian population, that of the Western-educated, largely urban elite that still controls the media and the school system of modern India. Through this group, the ideas of the early reformers trickle into the diverse religious life of village India.

mohandas gandhi

Gandhi was an extraordinary and unique man shaped by both his excellent Western education in England and his Hindu faith. He became one of the most influential leaders of the Indian independence movement by centering himself in Hindu beliefs, especially those expressed in the Bhagavad Gita. He interpreted this Hindu classic not as history, but as an allegory (a symbolic story that expressed truths about human life), especially its seeming acceptance of war. Gandhi's guiding principle in his religious and political life was the ancient Indian idea of *ahimsa* (non-injury). Gandhi and his followers resisted British rule without the use of violence. They were opposed to injuring anyone, even their enemies. Even though they were clubbed and beaten during demonstrations, they did not fight back. Gandhi believed his principle of non-violence could overcome anything, including the violence of others and even the power of the British empire. And he was successful.

In the following excerpt, Gandhi spoke about the Bhagavad Gita's teaching on non-attached action:

> The *Gita* says: "Do your allotted work but renounce its fruit—be detached and work—have no desire for reward and work."
>
> This is the unmistakable teaching of the Gita. He who gives up action falls. He who gives up only the reward rises. But renunciation of fruit in no way means indifference to the result. In regard to every action one must know the result that is expected to follow, the means thereto, and the capacity for it. He, who being thus equipped, is without desire for the result and is yet wholly engrossed in the due fulfillment of the task before him is said to have renounced the fruits of his action.

Gandhi had a political and religious task before him, winning independence for India and representing Hinduism in light of the Gita's teaching about detached action directed toward a result. As it was Arjuna's *dharma* in the Gita to fight with detachment toward the result of killing his enemies, it was the *dharma* of Gandhi and his followers to demonstrate non-violently and with detachment toward the result of overthrowing British rule in India.

eight

HINDUISM IN THE UNITED STATES

Hinduism spread to the united states in three ways: with the interest of nineteenth-century American intellectuals and philosophers—such as Ralph Waldo Emerson—who believed non-European cultures had something to offer the West, with the immigration of South Asians who brought their faith with them, and with Hindu teachers such as Vivekananda who toured the United States.

Many Euro-Americans (Americans of European descent) converted to Hinduism through the Vedanta Society, which continues to offer lectures on Hindu philosophy and study programs based on classical Indian religious texts, and which encourages personal devotion (*bhakti*). The society developed religious services modeled on Christian customs which included hymns, scripture readings, prayers, and sermons. Part of its teaching was that all people possess a divine nature that they should develop, and it offered the option of monastic vows. The Vedanta Society had great appeal to upper- and middle-class Euro-Americans and eventually to some Asian-Indian immigrants as well.

Additionally, in the 1940s many Americans were impressed by newspaper accounts of Gandhi's non-violent campaign for Indian independence. His example particularly influenced leaders of the American civil rights movement, such as the Reverend Martin Luther King Jr., who admired Gandhi and practiced non-violent resistance to draw attention to the laws that denied civil rights to all Americans. In later decades, other leading sources in the popularization of Hinduism among Euro-Americans were the colorful and talented spokesmen of the counterculture of the 1950s, 1960s, and early 1970s—like Aldous Huxley, Jack Kerouac, Allen Ginsberg, and the Beatles. In individual ways, all of these men promoted Hindu philosophy and beliefs in their books and music.

paramhansa yogananda

Paramhansa Yogananda was also important in the spread of Hinduism in the West. He came to the United States in 1920 and stayed for thirty years, founding the Self-realization Fellowship, which was based on yoga. He taught that if people could unite the divine spark within, or the Atman, to the universal Brahman (the spirit of the universe) they would achieve peaceful, successful, and healthy lives. He emphasized the physical practice of yoga to release tensions, breath control for calming the mind, and meditation to attain a state of oneness with the divine. Yogananda used Western psychological concepts to explain the basis of yoga in scientific terms. He created a Sunday service as well. A large part of his success can be attributed to his popular and well-known *Autobiography of a Yogi*, the simple yet moving story of his life.

maharishi mahesh yogi

The influence of Yogananda and Vivekananda on American society can be seen from the 1960s onward in the rising popularity of yoga, which was taught in community centers and on television. In 1959 Maharishi Mahesh Yogi introduced Transcendental Meditation, or TM as it is called. TM emphasized the measurable benefits of meditation like lowered blood pressure, reduced stress, and increased mental abilities. Two 15- to 20-minute sessions of Transcendental Meditation every day were recommended, using a secret mantra that was given to each individual during an initiation ceremony. The Maharishi attracted many celebrities and rock stars who made long visits to his *ashram*, or religious center, in India. Because of that, he received an enormous amount of news coverage.

Hari Krishnas

A particularly visible form of Hinduism in the United States is the International Society for Krishna Consciousness (ISKCON) founded in 1965 by A. C. Bhaktivedanta Swami Prabhupada (1896–1977). He taught an intense form of *bhakti* devotionalism focused on Krishna and based on the teachings of Chaitanya. The Hari Krishnas, as they were popularly called because of their continual chanting of the Hari Krishna mantra, sang and danced through the streets and airports of the United States wearing orange robes and with shaved heads. The Hari Krishna movement made no concession to Christian ideas about religion, and many Americans were shocked by the image of young Westerners who accepted the requirement of total surrender to the organization and its monastic practices of vegetarianism and celibacy. Financial and other scandals undermined the organization and its membership has declined, especially its Western membership.

After the passage of the United States immigration law of 1965, large numbers of South Asians immigrated to the United States. The vast majority of them were educated professionals or had studied at American universities and decided to stay and become citizens. Once settled in the United States, they wanted to teach Indian culture to their children, and they had enough money to do so. They built temples that also served as cultural centers that supported the arts and languages of India. Despite many Hindu sects and dialects, Indian communities in the United States pooled their resources to build temples that, in a gesture to accommodate various Hindu communities, included all the major Hindu deities. Temples dedicated to one god, which are so popular in India, are rare in the United States. American temples also modified their ritual calendars to take advantage of American secular holidays that become long weekends. An important difference between Asian and Indian American Hindus is that the latter claim they do not worship idols, a departure from the traditional Hindu belief that a god is present in his or her image. Yet once the statue of a deity is ritually dedicated, some Indian Americans believe that the god is present in the statue.

Today Hinduism, in its many varieties, is an established religion in the United States and is practiced in many temples and retreat centers. Yet, for the most part, a breach remains between the Hinduism brought over by Asian immigrants and the Hinduism of its Western practitioners. For people of south Asian descent, Hinduism is part of their cultural heritage, and they have little interest in reaching out to the larger Euro-American community. Also, numerous Westerners have taken Hindu ideas completely out of context. For instance, they practice Hindu meditation but ignore Hinduism's moral and ethical teachings, or they divorce Hinduism from its cultural heritage and interpret the tradition freely. Examples of this lack of context are common on the Internet, in magazines, and in the many books found in the New Age section of bookstores. Quite a number of these publications distort the meaning of Hindu deities and practices. Consequently, Asian Americans feel that Euro Americans neither respect nor understand Hinduism, while Euro Americans feel that Asian Americans confuse Hinduism with Asian culture.

Hinduism is flourishing in the United States in many forms, and there is an enormous amount of information available on the Internet, some put there by Euro Americans, some by South Asian Americans, and some by Indians living in India, all of which is having an impact on Hinduism in America. All that can be said with certainty about the future of Hinduism in America is that its impact on American culture will continue to increase.

This sculpture of Vishnu is found at Perumal Temple in Singapore.

about 1500–900 B.C.E.

Composition of the early Vedas

about 900–500 B.C.E.

Period of composition of later Vedas and early Upanishads. The rise of Buddhism and Jainism.

about fifth century B.C.E.–fourth century C.E.

The Mahabharata was written.

third century B.C.E.–fourth century C.E.

Composition of the Laws of Manu

about 200 B.C.E.

Valmiki's Ramayana is composed.

about 100 B.C.E.–100 C.E.

Composition of the Bhagavad Gita.

about 300 C.E.–1000

The Puranas are composed.

about 700.

Rise of Tantra and *bhakti*.

1100s

Muslim conquests in India.

1600s

First European settlements in India.

1800s

The Hindu Renaissance.

1947

India gains its independence from England

bahimsa—Non-violence, non-injury.

Arjuna—One of the Pandava brothers, who speaks to Krishna in the Bhagavad Gita.

arthas—The four goals of life: *artha*, material needs; *kama*, pleasure, love; *dharma*, duty; and *moksha*, salvation.

Arya Samaj—Society of Aryan Believers, which claimed that the Vedas were monotheistic (based on the belief in one god) and that they contained all truth, even modern scientific ideas.

ascetic—A person who practices spiritual disciplines like meditation and fasting.

ashramas—The four stages of life: student, householder, forest dweller, and renouncer.

Ashoka—Emperor of India in the third century B.C.E.

Atman—The eternal self.

Bhagavad Gita—A text composed around the second to first centuries B.C.E. that reveals Krishna to be all the deities in one and who offers salvation to everyone who experiences a wholehearted and passionate devotion to god.

bhakti—Wholehearted devotion to god.

Brahma—The creator god.

Brahman—The basis of all reality, the spirit of the universe.

brahmanical religion—Sometimes called Vedic religion; the early religion of India when brahman priests dominated.

brahman—A hereditary male priesthood and a caste.

Brahmo Samaj—Society of Brahma, which focused on Hinduism as based on the belief in one divine principle.

cakras—Means "wheels" or "circles"; mystical points or centers in the subtle (imaginary) body.

Chaitanya—A saint (1486–1534) influential in the worship of Krishna.

caste system—A social system of distinct classes into which people are born and remain for life.

Dassehra—The festival that celebrates Rama's defeat of Ravana.

dharma—Duty, law, religion.

Divali—The festival that celebrates Rama's return home; also called the Festival of Lights.

Durga—The Great Goddess, known for slaying the buffalo demon, Mahisa.

East India Company—A British trading company that came to rule India.

guru—A spiritual teacher.

Hindu Renaissance—The nineteenth-century reinterpretation of Hindu culture.

householder—The second stage of life; being married and having children.

idolater—Someone who worships a physical object as a deity or representative of a deity.

Indra—The thunderbolt-wielding warrior god.

International Society for Krishna Consciousness (ISKCON)—Founded by A. C. Bhaktivedanta Swami Prabhupada to encourage Westerners and Indians to practice Hinduism.

Kali—The fierce goddess born from Durga's rage.

Kali age—The fourth and last age of the world before it is destroyed.

karma—The belief that all acts have consequences in this life and in future lives.

Krishna—An incarnation of Vishnu, who teaches Arjuna in the Bhagavad Gita and who is also worshipped as the playful cowherder.

kshatriya—The warrior caste.

Laksmi—The goddess of prosperity and Vishnu's wife.

Mahabharata—The Indian epic about the Pandava brothers.

mandala—Means "circle"; a circular sacred drawing.

mantra—A set of sacred syllables and Sanskrit words.

moksha—Salvation; defined as liberation or release from the cycle of rebirth.

Navaratri—The great festival of the goddess Durga.

Pandava brothers—The heroes of the Mahabharata.

Parvati—The goddess who is married to Shiva.

pithas—Means "seats"; pilgrimage sites of the goddess Sati, wife of Shiva.

Prasad—Sanctified food that has been offered to the deity.

puja—Worship that includes making offerings to a deity.

Puranas—A collection and retelling of ancient stories about the gods, saints, and kings.

purdah—The Muslim practice of veiling a woman's face and keeping her in seclusion.

Purusha—The person from whose body the gods created the world.

Radha—One of the cowherding girls who is greatly loved by Krishna. She is a devout believer.

Rama—An incarnation of Vishnu.

Ramayana—Indian epic about Rama and Sita.

Ravana—In the Ramayana, the demon king of Sri Lanka who kidnaps Sita.

reincarnation—The belief that people are reborn.

renouncer—A person who has abandoned all family ties and possessions and lives as a wandering ascetic.

rita—The cosmic order.

Self-realization Fellowship—The organization founded by Yogananda enabling Euro-Americans to practice Hinduism.

shakti—The energy and power of Shiva; also the goddess as energy.

Sikhs—Followers of the religion founded by Guru Nanak, a blend of Hindu *bhakti* and Sufi mysticism.

Shiva—The god who creates and destroys the universe.

shudra—The laboring caste.

subtle body—An imaginary bodily system believed to influence physical and spiritual well-being.

Sufism—The mystical form of Islam that seeks union with God.

Tantra—A sect of Hinduism that worships fierce and terrifying deities, such as Shiva and the fierce forms of goddesses like Durga and Shakti. It stresses achieving enlightenment in one lifetime.

Theosophical Society—An organization founded to study ancient world religions and to derive from them a universal ethical code.

tilak—A lucky red mark placed on the forehead.

Transcendental Meditation—A movement founded by Maharishi Mahesh Yogi to promote meditation and Hinduism among Westerners and Indians.

Upanishads—Early philosophical writings of India.

vaishya—The merchant caste.

Vedanta Society—An organization founded by Vivekananda to educate, convert, and provide a spiritual community for Euro-Americans.

Vedas—The earliest Indian religious texts; a collection of hymns and prayers to various gods and goddesses, epic chants, and magic spells.

Vishnu—The god who preserves the universe.

yantra—Means "support"; a sacred drawing.

BOOKS

Albanese, Catherine L. *America: Religions and Religion.* 2nd ed. Belmont, CA: Wadsworth Publishing Company, 1992.

Bharati, Agehananda. *The Tantric Tradition.* New York: Samuel Weiser, 1975.

Bloomfield, Maurice, trans. *Hymns of the Atharva-Veda.* Oxford, England: Oxford University Press, 1897.

van Buitenen, J. A. B, trans. *The Mahābhārata.* Chicago: University of Chicago Press, 1975.

Coburn, Thomas B., trans. *Devī-Māhātmya: The Crystallization of the Goddess Tradition.* Delhi, India: Motilal Banarsidass, 1984.

Dimock Jr., Edward C., and Denise Levertov. *In Praise of Krishna: Songs from the Bengali.* Garden City, NY: Anchor Books, 1967.

Embree, Ainslie T. *The Hindu Tradition: Readings in Oriental Thought.* New York: Random House, 1966, 1972.

Falk, Nancy Auer. "*Puja*: Hindu *Puja*." *The Encyclopedia of Religion.* Vol. 12, pp. 83–85. New York: Macmillan, 1987.

Feuerstein, Georg. *Tantra: The Path of Ecstasy.* Boston: Shambhala, 1998.

Forbes, Geraldine. "Hinduism: Modern Movements," *The Encyclopedia of Religion.* Vol. 1, pp. 425–428. New York: Macmillan, 1987.

Freed, Stanley A., and Ruth S. Freed. *Hindu Festivals in a North Indian Village.* New York: Anthropological Papers of the American Museum of Natural History, 1998.

———. *Rites of Passage in Shanti Nagar.* New York: Anthropological Papers of the American Museum of Natural History, 1980.

Gold, Ann Grodzins. *Fruitful Journeys: The Ways of Rajasthani Pilgrims.* Berekeley: University of California Press, 1988.

Griffith, R. T. H., trans. *The Hymns from the Rig Veda.* Benares, India: E. J. Lazarus, 1920.

Haberman, David L. *Journey through the Twelve Forests: An Encounter with Krishna.* New York: Oxford University Press, 1994.

Hawley, John Stratton. *At Play with Krishna: Pilgrimage Dramas from Brindavan.* Princeton, NJ: Princeton University Press, 1981.

Hawley, John Stratton, and Mark Juergensmeyer, trans. *Songs of the Saints of India.* New York: Oxford University Press, 1988.

Jones, Kenneth W. *Arya Dharm: Hindu Consciousness in 19th-Century Punjab.* Berkeley: University of California Press, 1976.

Kinsley, David. *Hindu Goddesses: Visions of the Divine Feminine in the Hindu Religious Tradition.* Berkeley: University of California Press, 1986.

McDermott, Rachel Fell. "Kālī's New Frontiers: A Hindu Goddess on the Internet." In R. F. McDermott and Jeffrey J. Kripal, *Encountering Kalī: In the Margins, at the Center, in the West.* Berkeley: University of California Press, 2003, pp. 273–295.

Narayanan, Vasudha. "Creating South Indian Hindu Experience in the United States," in Williams, Raymond Brady, ed. *A Sacred Thread.* New York: Columbia University Press, 1966.

———. "Hinduism: In the West." *The Encyclopedia of Religion.* Vol. 1, pp. 428–430. New York: Macmillan, 1987.

O'Flaherty, Wendy Doniger. *Asceticism and Eroticism in the Mythology of Śiva.* Delhi, India: Oxford University Press, 1975.

Olivelle, Patrick. "Rites of Passage: Hindu Rites." *The Encyclopedia of Religion.* Vol. 12, pp. 387–393. New York: Macmillan, 1987.

Padoux, André. "Hindu Tantric Literature," *The Encyclopedia of Religion.* Vol. 6, pp. 365–367. New York: Macmillan, 1987.

———. "Tantrism: Hindu Tantrism," *The Encyclopedia of Religion.* Vol. 14, p. 274–280. New York: Macmillan, 1987.

———. "Tantrism: An Overview," *The Encyclopedia of Religion.* Vol. 14, pp. 272–274. New York: Macmillan, 1987.

Peterson, Indira Viswanathan. *Poems to Siva: The Hymns of the Tamil Saints.* Princeton, NJ: Princeton University Press, 1989.

Richman, Paula, ed. *Many Rāmāyanas: The Diversity of a Narrative Tradition in South Asia.* Berkeley: University of California Press, 1991.

Roy, P. C., trans. *Mahābhārata.* Calcutta, India: Bharata Press, 1883-1890.

Sircar, D. C. *The Śāktā Pīthas.* 2nd ed. Delhi, India: Motilal Barnasidass, 1973, 1998.

Stutley, Margaret, and James Stutley. *Harper's Dictionary of Hinduism: Its Mythology, Folklore, Philosophy, Literature, and History.* San Francisco: Harper & Row, 1984.

Williams, Raymond Brady, ed. *A Sacred Thread: Modern Transmission of Hindu Traditions in India and Abroad.* New York: Columbia University Press, 1996.

Wolpert, Stanley. *A New History of India.* New York: Oxford University Press, 1977, 1981.

FILMS
COMMERCIAL FILMS:

Devi. 96 mins, black and white, 1961. A film by India's greatest director, Satyajit Ray, takes place in Bengal during the Durga festival and tells the story of a young woman who is thought to be the Goddess.

Gandhi. Directed by Sir Richard Attenborough, color, 1982. Gandhi's life and fight for Indian independence.

The Mahabharata. directed by Peter Brooks, color 1990. Three- and nine-hour versions. www.paraabola.org/commerce.php

Mississippi Masala. Directed by Mira Nair, color 1992. Romance between an Indian girl and an African American boy.

Monsoon Wedding. Directed by Mira Nair, color, 2002. A young sophisticated and modern Indian boy and girl consider an arranged marriage.

The Ramayana. Made for Indian television, color.

Also, see the Bollywood section of DVD and Video stores, for popular films made in India.

DOCUMENTARIES

http://www.wisc.edu/southasia/films/index.html is the South Asian Area Center at the University of Wisconsin and is an excellent resource for renting or buying documentaries about India and Hinduism. For example:

Four Holy Men: Renunciation in Hindu Society. 37 minutes, color, 1976. Introduces four holy men or *sadhu*s who have renounced householder life, one of whom is from the Ramakrishna Mission.

Wedding of the Goddess. (Parts I & II) 36 and 40 minutes, color, 1975. Introduces the famous temple town of Madurai in south India and the twelve-day Chittari festival that celebrates the goddess Minaksi's marriage to Shiva.

An Indian Pilgrimage: Kashi. 30 minutes, color, 1969. Introduces the ancient and holy city of Varanasi, anciently called Benares and/or Kashi.

See also the list in the appendix by Sarah Caldwell in R. F. McDermott and Jeffrey J. Kripal. *Encountering Kali.* Berkeley: University of California Press, 2003, pp. 297–298, such as:

Ball of Fire: The Angry Goddess. Sarah Caldwell, 1999, 58 minutes. University of California Extension Center for Media and Independent Learning. A ritual from Kerala in which men impersonate and are possessed by the spirit of Kali.

Worship of God in the Form of Mother Kali. Adventures in Awareness, P. O. Box 5316, Fullerton, CA 92635. Kali worship at the Southern California Ramakrishna Mission temple.

WEB SITES

Ganesh Temple

http://www.ny/ganeshtemple.org

The Ganesha temple of New York has links to other temples in the United States.

The Hindu Universe

http://hindunet.org

General information and a wealth of links.

CHAPTER ONE:

pp. 10–11: "When Gods prepared the sacrifice . . ." R. T. H. Griffith, trans. *The Hymns from the Rigveda.* Benares, India: E. J. Lazarus, 1920, vol. 1, pp. 517–520.

p. 13: "Upon the earth men give . . ." Maurice Bloomfield, trans. *Hymns of the Atharva-Veda.* Oxford, England: Oxford University Press, 1897, pp. 201–204.

p. 15: "I extol Agni, the household . . ." Griffith, pp. 530.

CHAPTER TWO:

p. 18: "Out of the middle of the ocean . . ." Dimmitt and van Buitenen. *Classical Hindu Mythology,* p. 97.

p. 23: "'Across what is space . . ." *The Thirteen Principal Upanishads,* pp. 118–119.

p. 25: "He ran to It. It disappeared. . . ." *The Thirteen Principal Upanishads,* pp. 337–339.

CHAPTER THREE:

pp. 36–37: "Yudisthira said, 'Thou hast said . . ." P. C. Roy, trans. *Mahābhārata.* Calcutta, India: Bharata Press, 1883–1890.

CHAPTER FOUR:

p. 47: "Once she heard his name . . ." Indira Viswanathan Peterson. *Poems to Śiva: The Hymns of the Tamil Saints.* Princeton, NJ: Princeton University Press, 1989, p. 245.

p. 49: "'Know that that on which . . ." J. A. B. van Buitenen, trans., *The Bhagavadgītā in the Mahābhārata,* Chicago: University of Chicago Press, 1981, p. 75, 2.17–19.

p. 50: "When he sees me in everything . . ." van Buitenen, *The Bhagavadgītā,* p. 97, 6.30–32.

pp. 50–51: "If one disciplined soul . . ." van Buitenen, *The Bhagavadgītā,* p. 107, 9.26–34.

p. 51: "Katavur Virattam's Lord . . ." Peterson, *Poems to Śiva,* p. 42.

p. 52: "Hands, join in worship. . . ." Peterson, *Poems to Śiva,* p. 44.

p. 53: "I love him who dwells . . ." Peterson, *Poems to Śiva,* p. 227.

pp. 53–55: "Fingering the border of her . . ." Edward C. Dimock, Jr. and Denise Levertov, *In Praise of Krishna: Songs from the Bengali,* Garden City, NY: Anchor Books, 1967, p. 11.

p. 55: "As water to sea creatures . . ." Dimcock and Levertov, *In Praise of Krishna,* p. 17.

p. 57: "O Madhava, how shall I tell you. . . ." Dimcock and Levertov, *In Praise of Krishna,* p. 21.

p. 58: "When they had made love . . ." Dimcock and Levertov, *In Praise of Krishna,* p. 23.

pp. 58–59: "The honey of his look . . ." Dimcock and Levertov, *In Praise of Krishna*, p. 28.

p. 60: "Hare Krishna Hare Krishna . . ." John Stratton Hawley, *At Play with Krishna: Pilgrimage Dramas from Brindavan,* Princeton, NJ: Princeton University Press, 1981, p. 44.

p. 61: "Life without Hari is no life, . . ." John Stratton Hawley and Mark Jeurgensmeyer, trans., *Songs of the Saints of India,* New York: Oxford University Press, 1988, p. 135.

CHAPTER FIVE:

pp. 64–65: "The demon Mahisa himself, . . ." Thomas B. Coburn, trans., *Devī-Māhātmya: The Crystallization of the Goddess Tradition.* Delhi: Motilal Banarsidass, 1984, pp. 237–238.

p. 70: "He saw the goddess standing. . . ." *Devī-Māhātmya*, pp. 161–164.

CHAPTER SIX:

p. 75: ". . . at a human level . . ." André Padoux, "Tantrism: An Overview," *The Encyclopedia of Religion*, vol. 14, p. 274.

p. 78: ". . . produces, pervades, sustains, . . ." André Padoux, "Tantrism: Hindu Tantrism," *The Encyclopedia of Religion*, vol. 14, p. 277.

CHAPTER SEVEN:

p. 89: ". . . the West must learn to drink . . ." Embree, *The Hindu Tradition: Readings in Oriental Thought,* New York: Random House, 1966, 1972, p. 303.

p. 91: "The *Gita* says, 'Do your allotted . . .'" Embree, *The Hindu Tradition,* p. 342.

Page numbers in **boldface** are illustrations.

SERINITY YOUNG is a research associate in the Department of Anthropology at the American Museum of Natural History in New York City. She received her PhD in comparative religion from Columbia University in 1990 and has taught at Southern Methodist University, the University of Pennsylvania, and Hunter College. She has been a Fulbright Scholar, has been a fellow at the Center for Writers and Scholars at the New York Public Library, and has done fieldwork in India, Tibet, Nepal, Sri Lanka, Pakistan, Bangladesh, and Russia. She edited *The Encyclopedia of Women and World Religion* and *An Anthology of Sacred Texts by and about Women* and is the author of *Dreaming in the Lotus: Buddhist Dream Narrative, Imagery and Practice* and *Courtesans and Tantric Consorts: Sexualities in Buddhist Narrative, Iconography, and Ritual*.